Why Men Cheat
Truth Being Told

by Greg Wells Sr.

DORRANCE
PUBLISHING CO
EST. 1920
PITTSBURGH, PENNSYLVANIA 15238

Dorrance Publishing Co
585 Alpha Drive
Suite 103
Pittsburgh, PA 15238
Visit our website at *www.dorrancebookstore.com*

ISBN: 978-1-6470-2393-5
eISBN: 978-1-6470-2732-2

This book is dedicated in loving memory of my late, dear sister, Tabitha (Tabby) Colding.

Anthony! I love you, miss you, and will never forget you!!!

Chapter One
Allowing Him to Cheat

When will men stop cheating? When women stop settling for being the other woman.

Men make mistakes and fall short in the eyes of our significant others repeatedly before we get it right. Some guys will never get it right and will always be frowned upon as philanderers.

Many women voice their displeasure in the aforementioned behavior that a lot of guys around the world unveil. Yet it's some of these same women that involve themselves with these men knowing that the men are married or in active relationships.

Having knowledge that a man is married or in an active relationship and you as a woman opt to sleep around with him is the first mistake. At that moment, you're assisting him in cheating on his significant other. Aiding and abetting, contributing to his wrongdoing. In other words, you're allowing him to cheat.

Some of these same women are prevalent in saying that all men are dogs. So what does that make these women that are knowingly walking these dogs, knowingly petting these dogs, knowingly feeding these dogs and knowingly sleeping with these dogs? When they know that these dogs have a woman at home?

No matter how many times that man tells you that he's unhappy in his marriage or relationship or that he's going to leave her to be with you, you as a woman have to make mature adult decisions.

If the marriage or relationship is really on the brink of being over, then the man should respect you as a woman and totally wash his hands of his previous situation before starting anything new with you.

More importantly, the woman should respect herself enough to not get involved with a man that's already with another woman.

Too many women in this world settle for being the mistress, chick on the side or available only when the man wants them.

Things are good for you in the early stages. You can do whatever with him, then send him back home to his spouse.

It's all fun and games until you catch feelings. That's when the drama begins. Because now you're pressuring him to make good on those empty promises that he had been feeding you about leaving her to be with you.

Of course, he will find ways to manipulate you, buy you more gifts, tell you some more of what you want to hear and divert your attention from his true intentions. Which is just to continue to string you along, enjoy you at his own leisure and keep you a secret.

How can you complain when you as a woman knowingly engaged yourself in this situation with a man that you knew was already involved with another woman?

One thing women need to learn about a man is that regardless of the sweet talking he feeds you, a man will treat you the way he meets you.

So if a man lets you know upfront that he's married or in a relationship and you decide to mess around with him, regardless of what he tells you, you will never honestly have the respect of that man. You're simply playing yourself if you believe otherwise.

Yes, a man will tell you that he loves you and anything else you want to hear to keep you within arm's reach whenever he gets the urge for you. If you're a willing participant, that merry-go-round will be incessant until the situation comes to a head.

All the while that the husband and his mistress or the man and his side chick are having their pleasure-filled fun in the dark, creeping and keeping secrets, no one is concerned with the outcome of when the wife finds out or the girlfriend finds out.

It's a situation that many women turn a blind eye to until they are the wife or girlfriend themselves. Like they say, it isn't any fun when the rabbit has the gun.

Those women sleeping around with married men or guys that you know are in a relationship, I have some sound advice for you. If you ever want to be faithfully married or in a committed relationship with a man, then don't ever be the other woman!

Before you decide to mess with a man that is married or in a relationship, put yourself in the shoes of the wife or the girlfriend.

Imagine another woman doing all the things with your husband or your man that you're doing with somebody else's husband or man. How would you feel?

Consider being home night in and night out not truly knowing where your man is or who he's actually with.

Or he's coming home at odd hours with the same lame, tired excuses about why he didn't text you back or return your call.

Guys do what women allow them to. You have to respect yourself if you ever want a man to. Throw yourself at a married man or make yourself accessible to him whenever he wants you, then don't ever expect that man to honestly respect you as his woman or truly make you his wife.

Even if a guy does leave his wife or girlfriend for you, remember, he cheated with you on his wife or girlfriend. So what makes you believe your situation with him will be any different?

This is a guy that you allowed to have his cake and eat it, too. And that's how he will always carry you.

Too often women get caught up in listening to what guys tell them as opposed to seeing what he's showing them.

Ladies, you have to learn to listen with your eyes. A mouthpiece can have you believing the impossible. And we all know that physical pleasure can have a woman jumping through hoops for a man.

Another mistake that women make is believing that because a man is with another woman that she can just sleep with him and not have any ties to him. It starts out that way. Yet how often does someone in the situation begin to feel a certain way and want more?

The guy already has someone at home that he's still intimate with, which is why you're a secret in the first place. If you're creeping with a man and nothing about your arrangement with him is public, then yes, you're a secret.

Here's a couple of questions for you to ask yourself, ladies. How will a man respect me when I'm not respecting myself? Then ask yourself, are you giving that man something to respect?

Some women will say that they don't care what people think about them. That may be true with some. Those are usually the women that don't respect themselves and put their business out for everyone to know.

On the other hand, you have your women that are more discreet and like to keep their personal lives private. Either way you approach the situation, it's still wrong and wins you no genuine respect in the eyes of any man. Any man that tells you he respects you in that sense is lying to you and he has a motive. To get what he wants from you when he wants it.

Games can be run by either gender. Yet any woman that honestly believes in her heart that she's playing a man that's going home to another woman is certainly playing herself.

Whatever you receive from that man is a given. Whether it's pleasure or gifts. The fact is that he still goes home to his wife or girlfriend, still sleeps with her and has no intentions of leaving the stable environment that he's established at home to start all over with you when he already knows he can have you whenever he wants you.

It doesn't matter if that man buys you things, compliments you or makes you feel good. No matter how many times he tells you that he will, one thing he won't do is leave his wife for you!

A man will sell you a dream if you're gullible enough to purchase. Don't be so naïve and open to disaster. Hearts are fragile like glass and easily broken.

In reality, some women have heard so many lies from men that they no longer know what to believe. Not all married men or guys that are in a relationship are honest upfront. Sometimes women find out after already having slept with the guy or caught feelings for him that he's married or involved with another woman.

This is when a woman has the opportunity to make the right decision and sever all ties with this man.

Yet how many women honestly make the right decision when confronted with this scenario?

Those women that decide to lock in and deal with that man have to accept the heartbreak and anxiety that will follow. How rare is that, though?

Once feelings get involved, it's an entirely different issue. Forget what was agreed upon, you said, I said, etc., because now that four-letter monster is ringing forth problems that will have to be addressed and dealt with.

You agreed to secretly sleep around with this man and keep everything private between the two of you. Yet you lose your mind when things come to light and this man denies ever having been involved with you to his wife or girlfriend.

It comes with the very same territory that you were so disrespectfully treading on. Know the rules of the game and the consequences that come with getting involved before you sign on.

Once again, you were a secret and something to do at his convenience and that's a situation that you signed up for. Yes, he made you promises and told you he was going to leave her for you and so forth. Did you really believe that or were you just too caught up in the moment to even think?

If a man sincerely intends to leave his wife or woman to be with another woman, then he will leave that relationship completely before ever getting involved with another woman. If that's his true intentions.

Just make a mental note that the next woman that comes along like you could be the same reason he leaves you or sleeps around on you as well.

Surrendering your heart or mind to a man that's not totally committed to God is a disaster waiting to unfold. And know your place in that man's life before you start doing things for him like you're his wife.

'Cause if God isn't first in a man's life, neither will be his wife.

Chapter Two
Being Gullible

Allowing yourself to be manipulated into a compromising situation with a man can often be due to a woman being naive to a man's pure intentions in the beginning.

Not all guys are honest up front. There are many women around the world that can attest to that.

For example, you meet a new guy and he tells you that he's single. The two of you begin talking, dating and hanging out.

Little do you know, this guy has a whole woman at home. Some guys are even married. And that doesn't stop them from playing the field.

The thought doesn't cross your mind because he seems honest and the situation is fresh.

So you go with the flow because you don't want to run off the new guy. He's funny, makes you laugh, takes you out and he treats you nice. He's genuinely piqued your interest.

It's different than what you've been exposed to. He texts you before he goes to sleep, texts you good morning, even calls you throughout the day.

The two of you talk on the phone all day. His conversation is different. His focus is different.

Unbeknownst to you, you're actually serving as the balance to his relationship at home.

In a short period of time you've gotten hooked on the introduction. And usually the introduction isn't who the guy really is. It's how he presents himself to conquer what he wants.

So you've actually met his representative. And that's who you've fallen for.

It happens frequently with women that don't like to be alone, don't know how to be alone, just had their heart broken, been single for a while or didn't have a father figure in their life.

Each of them are vulnerable in a sense. And there are some guys who prey on specific women.

The insecure guy seeks naive women 'cause he knows she's easily manipulated.

Especially women that are involved in broken relationships that they don't see going anywhere.

These women see no potential for growth in their relationship. They desire more than what they're receiving from their mate at home.

Most of these women know that they're worth much more. Some flirt with the fantasies of being with another man that's more established than the guy that they're with.

In some cases, just 'cause she's entertaining it doesn't necessarily mean that she has intentions to act on it.

However, the women that open themselves up to the possibilities soon become targets for the opportunist guy.

As he senses her vulnerability, a vulnerable woman can be a needy woman. And that's what he wants. A woman that needs him in some capacity. Because then it's game on for him.

So he plays his role. Listening, giving sound advice, showing patience and understanding to her situation. Spending time with her, being there for her and filling that void that she had felt for far too long.

These are the types of women that are quick to invite a guy over to their house and open up their home to them. And these guys know that.

Some guys are only approaching you because they need somewhere to stay. Or she shows signs of being that naive female he can string along. Either way it mutually serves to his benefit. So he's heavy in pursuit.

Many women don't see that early on. As they get caught up in going with the flow, everything just seemed right. It's been a while since you've had a man in your bed every night. And you miss that.

So now you've moved him in. He's your man and you put up with all of his lying and cheating just so he won't leave you.

And why? 'Cause you love him and don't feel that you can do better? Or has he beat you down mentally, emotionally and stripped you of your dignity and sanity?

A man should challenge you mentally. Yet he should never abuse you mentally or emotionally.

Know the difference between being challenged and being abused. Don't be another victim.

Another common problem women run into is the physical attraction. This is a huge problem for many women.

Being physically attracted to a man can be one of the very reasons that a woman ignores the signs in the beginning.

Physical attraction can be misleading. So don't allow that to be the main reason you open up to a new guy.

Remember the common phrase, everything that looks good to you isn't necessarily good for you.

If he's a good-looking guy, chances are other women are attracted to him as well.

So ask yourself, is he a one-woman man? Is he honest? Is he loyal? Can I trust him? Ask questions of relevance.

Simple questions like, do you have children? If so, how many? Are they by the same woman? How old are they?

These are questions that should naturally come to mind in those early stages of dating someone new. And things that you should take the time to get to know.

For the cost of not taking the time to learn these things have been the major cause of many heartbreaks and broken relationships.

You can meet a guy that has two children the same age by two different women and completely ignore the fact that he had to be sleeping with two different women at the same time.

Some women will accept that this was his past without taking the time to probe and gain a better understanding of his dilemma.

There's also some women that have the attitude that he hasn't had a good woman yet and that's why he hasn't settled down.

You don't know how good those past women were to him. You only know what he has told you.

Now you believe that you're going to show him what a good woman really is. That's going to make a difference and he's going to treat you different?

Many women make the mistake of believing that because they're different than other women that'll make a difference with that same guy.

The fact that the two of you women are different is the very reason why he's messing with both of you!

It gives him a balance. How many times have you caught your man cheating and said, "This female isn't even on my level, she's nothing like me, she doesn't have nothing, isn't about nothing, she's ugly, how could you cheat on me with that, oh so you gon' cheat down" and so forth? You don't think he already knew that?

Of course he did. And that's why he was messing with her. She allowed him to do everything that you wouldn't. And she did everything for him that you wouldn't.

A guy doesn't consider the betrayal of his relationship until he's confronted with the reality of losing the woman that he loves.

This is a story heard too often around the world amongst guys. Yet once his woman forgives him and takes him back, it's not long thereafter that he's back cheating again. And more times than not, with that same woman!

There's nothing wrong with being single, ladies. Take the time to get to know yourself and what you really want. Learn your own triggers and pet peeves before getting involved with someone else.

Often in relationships, some women point fingers of blame at their significant other. When they, in fact, are the actual blame for the issues.

Owning up to your mistakes in a relationship is the mature thing to do. And two mature adults should be able to communicate and compromise.

Unfortunately, not every adult is mature. And effective communication does require maturity.

Lack of communication is also how a guy ends up talking to a woman outside of his relationship. He feels like she listens to him. And she understands him.

Sometimes it does start out innocent. It's just conversation. She simply listens to him vent. He doesn't see any harm in his actions because he feels they're just talking.

However, the more they talk, the more the two are transferring their personal energy to one another.

Not to mention the lack of respect that he's showing his woman by talking to another woman about their relationship. You should never vent to the opposite sex about problems that you're having in your relationship!

Situations like this involving a guy rarely ever have positive endings.

As attachments begin to form, the need to talk to the other person intensifies. What began as innocent simply because she would listen has become something more.

They start spending more time together. He's lying and giving excuses to his woman so that he can go hang out with the other woman.

By this time, he has become actively involved with the other woman. They're doing things whenever and wherever they can.

The other woman is comfortable with this arrangement. She knows he's in a relationship, knows he's not happy and she knows why he's unhappy in his relationship.

Therefore, she's going to be everything to him that his woman isn't. She's filling the void in his life because she has been giving the upper hand by a cheating man.

Meanwhile, the guy is now living a double life pleasing two women. He's lying to his woman at home. And telling the other woman part truth.

The other woman complies with the secret life and allows the guy to leave her time and time again to go home to his woman.

Most guys will be dishonest and tell the other woman that he's not sleeping with his woman at home, they're sleeping in separate bedrooms or they haven't been physical since he can remember.

This is where the other woman becomes gullible. 'Cause he makes time for her, spends time with her, buys her things, takes her places, pleases her, treats her good, she begins to treat him like her man.

She's loyal to him, doesn't talk to other guys and there's nothing that he could ask her to do that she wouldn't do.

Never mind the fact that he has a whole relationship that he goes home to when he leaves you.

Numerous women have truly been fooled to believe that they were in committed relationships with guys that had a woman at home. How can you commit yourself to someone that's already committed to someone else?

Especially those women that are dating married men. You know that he's married, yet you believe that you're in a relationship with him.

Is it because of the things that he does for you, how he treats you, how he makes you feel? Or is it because he's so honest with you and he doesn't lie to you?

He's basically doing what he has to do to keep you around. Spending money and spending time with you.

The mere fact that so many women are accepting of this behavior due to a man spending money and spending time with them is the very reason why so many guys will continue to wreck their own homes, wreck others' homes, manipulate masses of women and damage potentially good women.

Remember, it takes two to cheat. And people that cheat hate being cheated on!

Regardless of the reason given, it's the beginning of a never-ending cycle.

Some women complain about being lonely or having been single for too long. And they're eager to get involved with someone.

Having been single for an extended period of time and meeting a guy that she really likes can be one of the very reasons that a woman ignores the signs in the beginning.

Going without sex for a long period of time and telling yourself you'll just engage in physical pleasure with this new dude can mislead a woman into a trail of regrets.

Letting your guard down and trusting a guy that you haven't truly taken the time to get to know can be one of the very reasons that you ignore the signs in the beginning.

Just wanting to feel loved can certainly be a reason that a woman will ignore signs in the beginning.

Don't go seeking someone else to love you until you've adequately learned to love yourself first.

Everything about you begins within you. You can't truly be happy with someone else if you're not first happy with yourself.

No matter what a guy tells you, no matter what you see in him, you've got to see it in yourself first. Find your inner peace within you. Your happy spot can't come from a man and sustain the storms of life, if your light within isn't first turned on by you.

If you're going through a period in your life where you're doubting yourself and having insecurities, that's usually not a good time to get into a relationship with a guy. Stop thinking he can make things better for you. He's going to make things worse.

Take time to yourself to work on you. Allow the proper time needed to heal open wounds before even considering getting involved with someone new. Or you're putting yourself at higher risk to continue a painful pattern.

Your vulnerability will show to those that prey on the weak and wounded.

A man's status can also lead a woman to accept whatever comes with being with him.

Just remember, what attracts a man's attention doesn't always attract his respect. And what turns a man's head doesn't always turn his heart.

If you're dealing with a guy for what he has in his pockets, then you'll get what he has in his pants and not what he has in his chest.

Don't choose to be with someone simply for how good they look or how much they have. Choose someone that's going to treat you good and how much of themselves they're willing to give you.

Don't feel special when they're giving you time and attention because they're getting something from you. Feel special when they're giving you that same time and attention when they're not receiving anything from you.

Stop making yourself available for others at their convenience. And see if they treat you the same.

Chapter Three
Playing Yourself

No matter how much better you think you look than the woman that he's with, no matter how much harder you go to pleasure him, no matter how many different meals you can cook, none of that compares to the woman that a man's in love with.

Sure, you can have him physically. 'Cause a guy can love the woman that he's with and still cheat on her with other women. Yet his heart isn't available to any of those women. The saying is that you can get the stick yet his heart doesn't come with it!

Understand, fellas, the moment that you realize that your mind is single yet your heart isn't. That your lower extremities are available to other women yet your heart isn't. That your conversation is available to other women yet your heart isn't. Your time is available to other women yet your heart isn't. Simply means that you're not over your past and not ready to love someone else.

Therefore, you shouldn't be thinking, feeling or engaging a woman in that sense until you've taken the appropriate time needed to totally remove yourself from where you were. 'Cause it'll constantly prevent you from getting where you're supposed to be. Take time to yourself. 'Cause just like you're hurting others that are taking you seriously, you're seriously hurting yourself, by not first giving yourself what was appropriately needed. Time to heal.

Which is further damaging you internally and making you more toxic in your future relationships with women.

Ladies, you can't heal a guy that keeps using his pain as an excuse to hurt you. 'Cause if he hasn't healed what hurt him, he'll bleed on others that didn't cut him. And loving someone has never stopped them from cheating.

Guys cheat simply because they can. And not because they have to.

Many guys get caught up chasing temporary vagina, new vagina when they have good, loyal, and familiar vagina at home. Not understanding that you're leaving your woman vulnerable for any man to say the right things to the very lady that you're disrespecting and taking for granted.

Keep chasing what you think is better and neglecting the one that's truly in your corner, then accept it the same when you see another man holding down the very woman that you took for granted.

The little things that some guys take for granted today could be the big things they regret tomorrow. 'Cause some guys don't realize what they have until they no longer have it.

A cheating guy won't stop taking you for granted until you stop taking yourself for granted. Because they often take things for granted until it's taken from them.

Sometimes people don't feel what you feel until they feel what you felt. Take advantage of no one. 'Cause life deals you what you dish out.

Trying to pay someone back that hurt you is wasted energy. You can never get them back like karma can.

Temporary happiness isn't worth long-term pain. If you're truly unhappy where you are in your relationship, then start planning your exit.

There's a difference between giving up and knowing when you've had enough.

You'll never have anything real with someone that doesn't genuinely care about how you feel.

Consistency is the difference between having someone's attention or you had someone's attention.

Pain will teach you a lesson that pride won't allow you to learn. 'Cause love done made fools out of many people.

In life you can't lose what you never had, can't keep what's not yours and you can't hold on to someone that doesn't want to stay.

If life can remove someone you never dreamed of losing, it can replace them with someone you never dreamed of having. Don't be afraid to let go. You could be blocking your own blessings.

When God is showing you that someone isn't for you and you continue to be involved with them, He will make them hurt you continuously until you have no choice but to let go.

Don't waste time with people that don't serve a purpose in your life.

Invite them to church and see if they show the same interest as they do when you invite them to your bedroom.

A nice body will capture his attention. Yet it won't make him be faithful. You want a good loyal man, don't be eye candy, be soul food. He encounters eye candy daily. Separate yourself from the bunch.

True love isn't easy. And easy love isn't true. Love will break your heart. And hate doesn't make it feel any better.

So be careful what you open your heart to. 'Cause it's easy to give your heart to someone. Yet it can take longer than you have on this planet earth to get it back.

Trust should never be given. It should always be earned. Many relationships today are about as loyal as the people in them.

There's something wrong with your character if opportunity dictates your loyalty.

You'd think loyalty was a disease the way some people seem allergic to it. You can't make an honest person out of a liar. And you should never make a loyal person question your loyalty.

A guy doesn't become a man until he outgrows the boy in him. If having multiple women still excites him, he hasn't matured yet.

It takes a special man to love a complete woman appropriately. And not every man you meet will be that special man.

Chapter Four
Deceivers

Mistakes are often forgivable when people are honest and admit them. Yet it's no longer a mistake when people attempt to lie their way out of the situation.

Some guys will look you right in your face and lie to you. Then turn around and wonder why you don't trust them. 'Cause some still don't understand that when a woman is asking questions, she usually already knows the answers. She just wants to see if you'll be honest.

Yet not every guy claiming to be real is honest. And not every guy claiming to be honest is real. Don't walk blindly into situations. A lying tongue is also a cheating heart.

Living a lie is no different than telling a lie. And if you've got to question where you stand with someone, then you already have your answer.

No matter the situation, some guys just aren't going to be honest. They'll lie to you. Then turn around and expect the truth from you.

Don't allow comfort to keep you in an unhealthy relationship. Sometimes it's better to be uncomfortable than unhappy.

Allowing yourself to stay with a guy that you know is lying to you, that you know is cheating on you, only adds to your misery, self-pity and continued lower self-esteem.

Give no one that power and control over you. Your weakest moments are when you're supposed to be the strongest.

If you don't learn to love yourself first, you'll be chasing others that don't love you either.

Don't get caught up seeking loyalty in someone that doesn't truly love you. And it's impossible to receive true love from someone who isn't loyal.

Being loyal to someone that isn't loyal to you is like looking in the mirror and lying to yourself.

Just 'cause a guy desires you, that doesn't mean that he values you. If you respect yourself and value your worth, then you wouldn't settle for being anyone's secret.

Secrets don't remain secrets anymore. Guys brag to their friends about their encounters. And those same friends be pillow talking to their girl. Gossip travels faster than the truth.

Everything to your liking isn't what you need. And everything you need won't necessarily be to your liking. Don't get the two confused.

Many guys make time for what they want. And excuses for what they don't. You've got to do a better job deciphering the two.

When you're giving them attention and they're still seeking it from somewhere else, they're not playing you. You're playing yourself.

Especially those women that claim they only like bad boys. Then always crying about not being able to find a good man. The irony in that.

Ask yourself a question, if you kept your legs closed, would he care enough to find another way inside of you?

If the goal isn't to get married, what's the point of being in a relationship? What are you actually working towards?

Be careful who you open up to dating. Some of these guys aren't looking for love. They're looking for help.

There's someone out there searching for everything that you're giving someone that isn't appreciating it.

If the guy you're in a relationship with has a lock on his phone, then the two of you should be using condoms during intercourse.

If you have to sneak to do things, lie to cover it up, or delete it so it won't be seen, then you need to be single.

You can't reach for anything new if your hands are still full of yesterday's junk.

Some guys will pretend you're a bad person so they won't feel guilty about the things that they did to you. And the one accusing is usually the one doing it. Or looking for an excuse to do it.

If you don't want to be cheated on tomorrow, then don't be cheating today. What goes around always comes back around. And some guys aren't strong enough to handle that.

Treat the right guy wrong and you'll regret when you find out the wrong guy wasn't doing you right.

When you're angry with someone that you love, be careful what you say. 'Cause your mind is angry, yet your heart still cares.

Guys often say that there's more fish in the sea. However, if you knew how many times those fish have been thrown back in the sea, you'd keep your bait home, where it rightfully belongs.

The woman that you can't go a day without seeing, talking to and spending time with should be the only woman that you're seeing, talking to and spending time with.

Keep your family out of your relationship. And keep your friends out of your relationship as well. 'Cause they talk about you the most.

When you and the person that you're in a relationship with have a disagreement, don't involve your family or friends in your conflict. Remember, you may forgive them, and be right back in love with them. Doesn't mean that your family or friends will. Nor do they have to.

Same people that you'll give your last will be the first to stab you in the back. Turning their nose up at you and telling people how stupid you are to be back with him after all that stuff you said about him.

So if you don't want your business in the street, always keep it in house. If you can't talk to the person you're with, then you don't need to be with them.

Without communication there's no relationship. Without respect there's no love. Without trust there's no reason to continue.

Chapter Five
Lack of Discipline

To be wronged by someone only carries long-term effects when you choose to keep reliving it. Holding on prevents you from moving on.

Baggage is not attractive to a new relationship and it'll be a continued problem in an ongoing relationship. Take out your trash! You can't truly move on until you leave them alone!

To allow the wound to heal properly, you have to stop touching it. And stop asking people that haven't been where you're going for directions.

Keep giving your heart to people who live clumsy lives and you'll keep getting your heart broken.

Revenge isn't a wise game to be playing with your body. That "I only cheated because you cheated" mentality is so sophomoric. And it opens the door for even more problems.

Some females do cheat for revenge. They get upset because their man continues to cheat and show them no respect. She's hurting, tired of playing the fool and now she wants to get even.

However, chances are greater that the guy she chooses to seek retribution with isn't single or completely unattached either. He has a woman that he's already sleeping with or dealing with in some type of capacity. So to start dealing with the new guy, she's actually putting herself right back in the same position by dealing with a man that's talking to or possibly sleeping with another woman on the side.

Having someone on the side is a problem waiting to happen. No woman is opening herself up just to stay on the side while you enjoy a whole relationship at home with another woman.

Eventually the other woman grows to want more. And more than likely the guy that's cheating with her has been promising her that the two of them will be together.

Just keep in mind that if he cheats with you, then he'll cheat on you as well. What you accept is what you'll receive from a guy.

Fellas, the woman that you know that you can't live without is the one you should be doing everything to keep happy while you have her, not after you lose her.

Guys are simple beings. Not really that complex at all. Their thought process and decision making may really annoy you at times, ladies. 'Cause more often than not, guys truly do think with the wrong head.

A guy can love his woman, be a great provider, take care of all of the responsibilities that he's supposed to within his home and still cheat.

He doesn't have to be at odds with his woman to cheat. It doesn't have to be something she did or didn't do for him to cheat either.

Some guys will cheat simply because they're bored. As immature as it sounds, there's guys that really are that simple. Idle time isn't a friend to a man that lacks discipline. Idle time can be problematic for some guys.

The other head that guys possess likes to cum. And a guy will cheat simply because he's horny. They call it getting their nuts out of hot.

Crazy thing is, he doesn't even have to like the woman that he's cheating with. Doesn't even really have to be attracted to her. When he's horny, he just wants to cum.

That's why some guys have babies with women that they only intended to get their rocks off with.

Every guy has sleepers. Some call them creepers. They're women that guys don't want anyone to know that they slept with.

These women become known as homewreckers. 'Cause they'll sleep with your man whenever he wants and wherever he wants.

Having knowledge of that, many guys will continue to creep with these women under their own respective conditions.

You'd be surprised how many guys play the laws of averages simply because they know that women greatly outnumber men in society.

These particular guys aren't concerned with losing what some consider a good woman while they're doing what's pleasing to them.

Simply because they believe that there's more good women than there are good men out here. Many guys have messed over several good women in their lives and yet can still meet a good woman tomorrow that'll be everything a guy could ask for in a wife.

For ladies, that's not the case. If you get a good man, you try to be everything he desires to keep him home and happy. It just comes natural. Because you know the pickings are slim out there.

You've experienced enough by now to know that some guys look good to you, yet may not be good to you. He might say all the right things, yet do all the wrong things.

Which will open scars from your past. If you like being lied to, cheated on and playing games, then keep playing the field. Just remember, someone has to take the "L" in the end. 'Cause guys are quick to move on. And women hold on, due to emotional attachments.

It's easy to find someone to chill with. And much harder to find someone to actually build with.

Don't sacrifice the one that's holding you down for the one that's holding you back. Know the difference. If you're not growing and building together, then you're just chillin' together.

Any guy that would deal with a woman with no strings attached or open relationship is telling you what he thinks of you. You're a convenient screw. Any man that really cares about you doesn't want to share you with anybody.

Regardless of what they tell you, men are territorial creatures. So a man that loves you will be jealous. It doesn't make him no less a man either. It simply implies that he genuinely cares about you and doesn't want to share you with anyone.

Now to the guys who just want to get off when they want or be bothered with you when they want, they only care about what they want and when they want it from you. These types of guys are used to telling women what they want to hear to get what they want in return. After that guy comes, he doesn't feel the same way about you. Nor does he want to be around you. He's giving you excuses to leave or wants you to go if it's his place.

Problem is, many of you women know that if you don't give it to him, then he'll go and satisfy his urges elsewhere.

This is where self-respect has to nullify what you think you share with him.

Fact of the matter is, he's not going to change. If not you, it'll be some other woman. You have to be strong enough to let it be that other woman then.

Now if you truly care for the man that you're in a relationship with and want things to work, then pleasing him regularly comes with the territory. If you don't, you know what you're opening the door to.

Chapter Six
Holding Out

One of the most common mistakes a lot of women in relationships make with guys are holding out when they're at odds with him.

Whether you thought he had a woman on the side or not, he will have one once you start withholding sex from him.

When a guy wants to release, that's what he wants to do. Guys aren't as strong as women in that aspect.

Some guys already have a woman they can connect with whenever there's trouble at home. She's always prepared to tighten him up when his woman is neglecting his needs.

She's aware of her role in his life. No explanation needed. He reaches out and she responds as he desires.

Now there are some guys who try to be strong and work things out at home with their woman. Through the arguing, disagreeing, silent treatment and holding out.

Yet eventually they too fall victim to obtaining from another woman what they're not getting at home from their woman.

Outside of the physical element, men are yet but so strong willed at resisting temptation. And will wait so long for a woman to give them what they desire.

Keep in mind, ladies, you're depriving him of simple pleasures that he's being offered daily from random females and turning down while waiting for you.

A lot of women are baffled when their man gets tired of waiting for them and begins accepting those offers from other women.

It doesn't make it right that guys do it. No, not by any means. It's your body and you have the right to grant or deny any man access whenever you so choose to.

Just understand that neglecting the physical needs of your man can be the very reason that he begins cheating on you.

Often some ladies find out that their man is cheating on them. So they break up with them. You yell at him, curse him out, tell him you hate him, put him out, say you'll never forgive him and so forth.

Yet as time passes by, she begins to miss him. She's thinking about him. Wondering what he's doing. And she doesn't want the other chick to have him either.

So she ends up getting back with the guy that cheated on her. However, she's still harboring hatred towards him for cheating on her.

Therefore, she's reluctant to his touch and physical advances. So once again, you're holding out on him.

You took him back. Yet you're still not giving him what he desires. Then you get angry when he resorts back to the same cheating behavior that he was exhibiting before.

Ladies, you should take the necessary time needed to heal before engaging yourself with the man that hurt you. 'Cause if you don't and you're not truly over it, chances are greater that you're not ready to jump right back in bed with him.

Yet when you call him up and tell him that you want him back in your life, that's what he's thinking. 'Cause guys are simple creatures.

You've forgiven him, he's apologizing and saying that he'll never hurt you again. You want to believe him. Yet that shadow of doubt and betrayal still weighs on you ever so often.

Yes, you've forgiven him. Yet you want to take things slow. 'Cause the trust needs to be rebuilt. That's not how all guys see it, though.

So his advances towards you are met with resistance early on. You want to talk about why he cheated on you. He keeps saying, "I apologized, I'm sorry, can't we just get past this already?"

You want to talk about it. And he doesn't. You feel he doesn't understand how much he hurt you, betrayed you and made you feel insecure.

To you, the mere fact that you've even taken him back says that you want to hear why he did it, for him to say that he was wrong, apologize to you and you will be able to believe him. Yet he needs to give things time.

In his eyes, the fact that you've taken him back means that you forgive him, you love him and things are back to normal.

So when he's trying to initiate intimacy with you and you resist, he doesn't understand that mentally and emotionally you're not there. And that's not what you want or need from him right now.

His lack of understanding what's needed of him as a man that has done wrong by his woman eventually leads him back to cheating on her again.

Ladies, I know there are various reasons as to why you don't want to be intimate with your man. And sometimes you actually can't.

Things happen with your body. You go through mood swings and changes that he wouldn't understand. And it's often more mental for some ladies anyway.

Every guy doesn't process and retain information the same. They definitely don't think the same either.

So you can explain to the man that you're in a relationship with why you're not interested in intimacy with him at the time and instead of him comprehending and working towards a mutual solution with you, he's turned off, upset and low-key already set his sights on fulfilling his needs elsewhere with another woman.

It speaks volumes about the maturation level of the man you're involved with, his genuine love and overall concern for you.

Problem is, so many women get wrapped up in what they feel for their man that they don't see his lack of respect, care or concern for them.

Which leads to heartbreak, depression, low self-esteem, lack of self-confidence, questioning your own self-worth and sometimes even blaming yourself for his shameful actions.

Ladies, you don't push your man to cheat. He chooses to cheat! And a woman holding out on her man requires maturity, patience and understanding from him as to why.

Not all guys are the same. Some will understand, support you and stand by your side faithfully.

On the other hand, you have the callow individuals that use it as an excuse to cheat. And in most cases, they were already cheating anyway. So don't stress yourself out over something that you can't change, the choices of a man.

Chapter Seven
Out the Rut

If you're not ready to commit, then why would you as a responsible male adult get involved in a relationship?

Ladies, you've got to initially start requiring more from guys. Jumping into bed and these shaky relationships without learning the direction he has in mind for the two of you to go is wasted time and possibly years of regret.

Not every guy has a good heart. All guys' intentions aren't always honest. And some guys' words conflict with their actions.

Ladies, the failed relationships that you've had was life's lessons of what you don't want in a man. Yet if you keep fishing in that same lake expecting to catch one good fish, then you'll have that same misery, heartbreak and pain to endure all over again.

Maybe you should throw that old pole in that contaminated water, stop fishing and become the bait in another location. Unless insanity is your middle name.

Dwelling on your past could cause you to be a prisoner of your past. What could've been isn't for a reason. And what didn't happen wasn't supposed to happen.

When God closes a door, don't question why. You never know how detrimental things would've been. Appreciate what and who you do have in your life without always questioning why.

Fellas, if your woman is paying the bills, then don't call yourself the man of the house. A man holds down a job and his household without having being told to.

- You don't have to tell a man to be a father.
- You don't have to tell a man to be a MAN.
- You don't have to tell a man to be a provider.
- You don't have to tell a man to be a protector.
- You don't have to tell a man to be faithful.
- You don't have to tell a man to be honest.
- You don't have to tell a man to get a job.

Because a man is naturally a provider. Wise and mature in heart, spirit and mind. So all of the above comes naturally to him.

Fellas, anything that you don't want your woman doing, you shouldn't be doing. Everything that you want to do isn't necessarily what you need to be doing.

For instance, fellas, the next time you're jumping up and down in someone else's girl, picture someone else jumping up and down in your girl the same.

Picture her having another man all in her mouth the way she does you. Don't get mad, you've got your face buried all in between some other female's legs.

Just 'cause she doesn't leave you doesn't mean she's not out getting even! Some women don't forgive you until they've gotten revenge. So if you've done wrong by your woman, she's forgiven you and taking you back, chances are greater that she's already gotten even or planning to.

No matter how many times she tells you in the heat of the moment that it's yours, you don't own no vagina! If God intended for you to own a vagina, He would've given you one.

To the ladies that are loyal and seeking the same in your man, one of the sad battles that you're up against is that it's so many females that will accept him any way that they can have him.

Then you get mad at the females, and for what? Because she knew that was your man? You often get caught up in your emotions and neglect the one that really owes you respect in the situation.

Your man owes you trust, honor and respect to not be cheating on you. She didn't take the "D" from him. And she's certainly not having text conversations with herself either.

As we grow, we learn. So we learn as we grow. Experience is often spoken to be the best teacher. What you go through should therefore be both your guide and example of what not to continue to allow or accept in your life.

Put your hand on a hot stove and get burned, you won't do that again. Jump in deep water and can't swim, you won't do that again.

Yet to love and get hurt repeatedly by the same person, then keep asking why is your choice to continue playing Russian Roulette with your heart. Think about it.

Be honest with yourself. The first person that you don't owe a lie to is yourself. Don't allow what other people think of you to determine who you feel you have to be either.

Remaining in a relationship that has become stagnant just to save face with people around you is pain not worth enduring.

If their daily presence in your life isn't serving any meaningful purpose, their immediate absence should be required.

When going through your personal storm you experience many ups, downs, get betrayed, deceived, lied to, lied on, misled, manipulated and many other negative things that keep you in that forbidden rut.

Many broken promises from guys that never materialize. Guys say they have your back, you turn around and unfortunately he's not there.

When you're fighting through the adversity with every ounce of energy you have to continue climbing to the top of that mountain and it seems that those at the top are yelling obscenities at you, putting you down, laughing at you, making a mockery of your situation and telling you that you'll never make it to the top of the mountain, where they're standing oh so proudly.

When you finally achieve your goal, everything you went through to get there and all that you have endured from your painful relationship should be the reason you forgive and let go.

Speak in a positive sense to others when going through their own personal storm in attempts to make it out of their own dilemmas. It's always better to encourage.

Not everyone's struggle will be the same. Nevertheless, hardships and hard times in any sense are real.

No matter what you've been through or going through, don't allow what someone else feels, thinks or says to discourage the will inside you to keep climbing out of the rut.

Chapter Eight
A Fool's Pride

Most guys don't know the difference between a penny, a nickel or a dime. To some guys, a couple nickels equals a dime. To some guys ten pennies equals a dime. It all equates the same to them.

A man knows there's no substitute for that one woman that's a couple nickels or ten pennies herself.

She wants a man she can truly call her own. Then she'll treat you like a king on his throne.

However, you can't expect to be treated like a king if you're not going to respect your queen! Royalty is loyalty in your castle.

Don't give her reasons to be insecure. She should find security in her man in every way that a woman seeks it in her man. Be a complete man, not just the meat man.

If you're not EVERYthing that he wants, don't be SOMEthing they can have, ladies.

If their actions don't match what they're telling you, don't be oblivious to keep buying what they're selling you, ladies.

- Love doesn't hurt.
- Love doesn't hate.
- Love isn't jealous.

- Love isn't insecure.
- Love doesn't cheat.
- Love doesn't lie.
- Love isn't angry.

Yet if you make someone that loves you angry by continuing to lie to them, cheating on them, causing insecurities, making them jealous, that will eventually cause them to feel like they hate you, in turn causing them to attempt to make you feel the same hurt that they feel.

A guy that messes around with a woman knowing that she has a man doesn't respect her at that point and won't respect her after.

Even if she leaves her man to be with him. You cheated on your dude to be with him. So you'll never genuinely have the respect of that man.

Nor will any woman that messes with a married man or a guy that's in a relationship.

Once you settle for being the other woman, you lose respect and value in the eyes of that guy. You're worth the pleasure you can provide him with and nothing more.

You want them to be everything you desire in a relationship, then you have to be everything they desire in return. The two of you feed off one another.

Fellas, if you truly love your woman, don't just tell her that you love her. Show her that you love her!

Make her feel loved and appreciated. Don't take her for granted. 'Cause there's always another man waiting to catch what you drop. And they will appreciate her the way you should have. And treat her the way you should have. And on most occasions, the male ego won't receive that well.

Treat every day you spend with her like a gift. Don't take anything about her for granted. 'Cause as sure as she has been placed in your life, she can be taken from your life without warning.

Appreciate what's given, cherish the moments and create memories worth remembering together.

Because nothing lasts forever, except time. Which none of us can control. And time can be your enemy if you don't use it wisely.

Pride will keep some guys from apologizing to their woman when they're wrong. Pride will keep some couples from talking to one another while living under the same roof.

Pride will prevent couples from working out compromising solutions and forgiving one another. Pride will make an honest tongue tell a lie!

Pride can also be the reason a couple doesn't maximize their potential together. Pride can be the reason you lose someone that you can't get back as well.

Don't allow your pride to be the reason that you live in a state of adamant ignorance and regret.

Emotionally led decisions are often the ones guys regret the most. Guys are quick to act on what they felt at the moment. Only to later regret it. That's one of the reasons why they say that cooler heads prevail.

Give yourself time and space necessary to weigh out the consequences of your thoughts, words and actions before you place yourself in an uncompromising position with your woman, fellas.

There are guys that lost truly good women that wish they exercised this simple method beforehand. Trouble can be easy to get into and difficult to get out of.

So be slower to anger and quicker to forgive, fellas. What your lady says that pisses you off could be the same thing that both of you are laughing at a couple days later. Exercise a bit more patience and understanding with her.

Indeed, some females are just going to act ignorant regardless. Yet keep in mind, who's more ignorant, the one who starts it or the one who responds?

If you're above what's beneath you, walk like it! Your life isn't a video game, so don't play with it. You get no do-overs and there's no reset button.

A lot of guys have either been in some situations within their relationship or had an ex taken from them due to the aforementioned immediate responses.

The end result causes more pain, stress and continued heartache than the initial action itself.

So if you value your time, don't continue spending it with anyone that you know isn't worth it. 'Cause you can't make them stay where their heart isn't.

A relationship in which you are not relating to the other person is wasted energy that you could positively be applying to something more relevant and meaningful with a purpose in your life. This definitely opens the door for stepping outside of your relationship as well.

All relationships have problems. It's how you communicate to solve those problems that dictates the outcome.

Chapter Nine
Happy Home

A man that cares will listen. A man that listens won't keep making the same mistakes. A man that's not making the same mistakes won't hurt you. A man that won't hurt you will take the time to love you.

A man that takes the time to love you will truly appreciate you. A man that truly appreciates you will always be there for you. A man that will always be there for you is the man that only wants to see you happy.

A man that only wants to see you happy will marry you and be the faithful, loyal soulmate that he sought and obtained in you!

Not play games with your heart, lie to you, manipulate you, lead you on and be cheating on you the whole time.

Ladies, you want to know if your man is out doing you filthy, send him a sexy message telling him what's waiting for him at home and if he isn't pulling up before you set your phone down, then your home is not the only place his pipe is laying.

Take the time to send her random text. Even if you're just letting her know that you were thinking about her.

Call her just to hear her voice. Listen when she vents. Kiss her, hold her and let her feel the warmth, comfort and care in your embrace. Your woman should feel safe from all stress and worries in your arms.

Don't just surprise her with gifts. Allow her to come home to peace and quiet, kids' homework already done, hot bath, candles, some relaxing music, her favorite wine and make sure all the bills are paid.

She wouldn't be nagging if you were doing as she was asking. Fellas, listen to your woman. It doesn't make you soft to listen to the needs of your woman. It makes you a man that understands and cares.

A man that loves his woman will keep her happy. When your woman's happy, your home is happy. Keep a smile on her face. You should always be the reason that she's smiling. Ladies, keep your man happy as well. Because it's not just happy wife happy life. It's happy spouse happy house!

Fellas, make the bed even if you're not the last one to get out of it. Help out around the house. Clean the tub/shower out. Cook dinner a few nights throughout the week.

Some days she's tired when she gets home. Ask her how her day was. Rub her feet. Give her a massage. Help her to relax. Make her feel special and appreciated.

Do the little things like wash the dishes. Take the trash out without her having to ask you to. Separate the clothes and throw a load in the wash.

Put gas in her car. Keep all of her maintenance up on her vehicle. Keep her car clean like you do yours, fellas. Cut the grass without her having to ask you to. Set a schedule and stick to it.

Get up and help get the kids off to school sometimes. Every month, all the bills in the house should be on the table.

To have a meaningful relationship that'll last, it requires two people that have an understanding. Two people that openly communicate, that are open to compromise.

Two people that both understand the bond of trust and the importance of maintaining it. Two people that are willing to listen to one another.

Two people that respect one another and can accept constructive criticism from one another. This is a problem in many relationships.

Two people that keep all issues within their relationship between the two of them.

Two people that openly communicate and are both financially responsible in their relationship.

Two people that are equally yoked and they take things to God, not social media, not their family and certainly not their friends.

Your happiness and security have to be a priority in a relationship or marriage. Otherwise, you're just playing house.

Apologizing when you're wrong shows signs of maturity, not signs of weakness. Life is a matter of choices, not excuses.

Advice is free. The decisions you make are what can be costly. Your spouse should be your friend, not your enemy.

A successful relationship takes two people, not one and certainly not three people. Only exception is God being in the equation.

When you're the only one caring, trying and giving in the relationship, it won't work.

Keep issues within your relationship between you and the person you're in a relationship with.

A successful relationship needs two people that are willing, forgiving, wanting, communicating, compromising, giving and accepting on one accord with God heading their households.

Chapter Ten
Neglecting His Needs

No matter how big their ego is, how secure they seem, how confident you think they are, how much money they have, how good looking they are, all men like attention, ladies.

Something as little as not giving him attention at home can have him seeking it on social media, in the club, at work, the grocery store, in church, online dating apps, you name it.

Pretty much anywhere his woman is absent and other women are present. Especially considering the fact that some guys like variety.

As petty as it sounds, it's one of the main reasons a lot of guys cheat. And it can start out as innocent as receiving the attention from another woman that he wasn't receiving from you.

Some guys are going to cheat no matter how much attention their woman shows them, no matter how good their woman is to them. 'Cause it's just who they are.

Well, this chapter isn't about those guys. This chapter is about the guys that start cheating due to what they desire from their woman at home yet aren't receiving from her.

Guys like to be complimented and feel like their efforts are appreciated at home. Don't take his actions for granted, ladies.

Saying that he's your man, he's supposed to do these things, is no different than a guy saying you're his woman, you're supposed to do certain things. And when you're not doing those things is usually when the cheating begins for most guys.

For instance, let's look at an example couple, William and his wife Keisha's relationship. William really loves his wife Keisha. He proposed to her after three months of dating. The two of them got married six months later.

They have two beautiful children together. He's an entrepreneur. Takes care of home, he's a good father, he doesn't run the streets and doesn't let his wife go without.

This is one guy that was a devoted husband and had never cheated on his wife. Not even when they were just in the dating phase.

Over the years, William and Mike had established a business together and became best friends. William confided in Mike about everything from problems with his family to issues within his marriage.

Being a good friend, Mike always listened to him vent. Then he'd simply reassure and redirect William in the most positive manner given the particular situation.

There truly were some trying times within their relationship where William held fast and remained faithful to his wife when most guys would've bolted and been out actively on the hunt for some fun on the side.

The first real test in their marriage came when Keisha had serious complications giving birth to their second child.

During the time that she was pregnant, William was right by her side at each and every doctor's appointment. The same way that he was during their first pregnancy. He was attentive, listened and paid precise attention to detail.

Even though they were expecting their second child, William would excitedly call Mike up telling him everything that the doctor said after each visit.

There were times that Mike couldn't believe that William really remembered word for word what was stated at the appointments. William could be very convincing, though.

Sometime around the third trimester was when Keisha began having some complications with her pregnancy. She was stressing a lot about it. And William dug in and gave his all at being supportive to his wife.

The difficulties with her pregnancy weren't the only issues that Keisha was dealing with at the time either.

Way back when Keisha was in middle school, her favorite aunt passed away while trying to give birth. That traumatized Keisha! She used to have nightmares about how her aunt passed. And she grew up vowing that she would never have any kids.

Early on in their dating stages, William would ask Keisha how she felt about marriage and having children. She had several opportunities to let him know about her past trauma and opted not to.

Instead she gave him all of the answers that he was looking to hear. Even agreeing with William, stating that she too wanted to have a big family.

The excitement grew quickly within him. William was wrapped up in how beautiful Keisha was, how intelligent she was, how independent she was and they shared so many common interests. The two hit it off tremendously.

Their nearly picture perfect marriage took a dramatic turn for the worse after Keisha survived the complicated birth of their second child.

A year after having given birth to William Jr., Keisha still hadn't been intimate with William in no way. She wouldn't even let him touch her!

Prior to her last pregnancy, the two were an easygoing couple that got along very well. Very seldom disagreed with one another about anything. And the two of them could talk about anything. Their marriage often seemed like a fairytale.

However, William says that recently she has become so distant. She doesn't say more than a few words in conversation. He tries to kiss her and she turns her head. He goes to hug her and she just stands there with her arms dangling to her side.

When he asks her what's the problem, is it something that he did, or something that he can do? She just replies, no, everything is fine. And he knows everything isn't fine with his wife.

However, without having full knowledge of what's going on inside of her, he's still standing beside his wife, praying that they make it through.

Each of his efforts and attempts at helping his wife get through what she had been going through was getting met with sheer resistance. She refused to go to counseling, stopped going to church and she even quit her job.

Without planning to do so, Keisha became a stay-at-home mom. William wasn't concerned with her not working and staying home with the kids because he was more than capable of being the sole provider for their household.

This was a very strong-willed man that honestly loved his wife. Mike frankly recalled how many times William sat on his couch crying that he didn't know what else to do.

Telling Mike that he had tried everything to get her to come around. And she showed no interest in any options or possible solutions that he brought to the table.

William also told Mike that he hadn't touched his wife since the birth of their son, she sleeps in full pajamas under a completely separate blanket with two pillows between them and dismisses any of his intimate advances. William said he looks at his wife and she just stares blankly at him.

One day, William looked Mike in his eyes and said, "She's treating me like I broke our vows and cheated on her!"

In response, Mike looked William in his eyes and asked him, "Have you ever cheated on your wife?" Sobbing heavily, William shook his head and said, "No!"

At that time Mike got up and poured both of them a drink. And Mike believed that he needed a drink more than William did at this point. Because it was difficult to see his good stand up friend in that state. William certainly didn't deserve the cold shoulder that he was receiving at home from his wife Keisha.

Mike's mind began racing at the possibilities of what could've triggered the sudden turmoil in their marriage.

Suddenly Mike was wondering, could this all be stemming from postpartum depression that William's wife was going through? Could this be long term? Would it have any effect on their child? Is he familiar with the medical term?

Thinking out loud to himself, Mike thought maybe he'd have William seek counseling on his own with a doctor that'd educate him on the possibilities of postpartum depression.

William sat there holding his drink for what seemed like an eternity. And hadn't even attempted to take a sip.

Until Mike finally decided to break his concentration. Mike cracked a simple silly joke. And surprisingly, it made William laugh.

Being that Mike had broken through, he proposed a toast to their friendship and always standing solid for one another whenever the other was in need.

Without thinking, William nodded his head in agreement and took his first drink of the night. It really loosened him up, too.

About a half-hour later, William was drinking straight out of the bottle and confessing the continued love and loyalty that he's maintained for his wife.

There were moments that William began laughing and expressing happy times that he's encountered with his wife. Talking about how great of a woman Keisha is, how great she is with their kids and how he's blessed to have her as his wife.

William's eyes lit up when he spoke about all of the great times he and his wife enjoyed with Mike and his wife.

For years now, both fellas were married and enjoyed many vacations and trips together accompanied by their wives. William and Mike were truly best friends. And their wives became girlfriends as well.

They both loved their wives and respectively headed their households. Yet this moment was about William and Keisha, not Mike and his wife Tabitha.

So as Mike channeled his attention over to his friend, William paused, looked at Mike and kept repeating, "Out of all of the men in the world, my Keisha chose me, she chose me, did you hear me, Mike, she chose me!"

Then William broke down crying, asking, "How could she be treating me like this, what did I ever do to deserve this treatment? I've never cheated on her! I've been a good, honest and faithful husband to her!"

William continued, "She's never had to worry about anything. I've never let her do without." Then he sat the bottle down on the table and said, "I just don't know what else to do!"

As William sat before Mike, rocking back and forth on the living room sofa, the whole time Mike sat there listening and nodding. Trying to be there for a friend in need. Mike sat there patiently, allowing William to get that good cry out that he had been holding in.

Once William began to regain his composure, Mike calmly let him know that he understood how he felt and why he felt the way he did.

Having knowledge of William and Keisha's recent chain of events within their home, Mike knew it was time to find a solution to their problem before it took an even more damaging turn for the worse.

Yet before Mike could speak, William interrupted him with a sarcastic laugh, saying, "Man, my bad for breaking down, crying and letting my emotions all out." Pounding his chest, he continued, "I'm not soft."

Then William picked up the bottle to take another drink and Mike took the bottle from him.

"You've had enough to drink for the evening," is what Mike told him. Then continued, "I've sat here and listened to you without interrupting you as an understanding friend should. Now you're going to sit here and listen to me without interrupting as a good friend should.

"First off," Mike said to William, "it doesn't make you soft because you love your wife and you're fighting to remain faithful to your marriage. It makes you a man! A man that any woman would respect, admire and love to call their own.

"Second, you remain diligent in your everyday efforts with your wife. Continue supporting her and being there for her. Temptation is a temporary desire easily overcome by a strong mentality. So be stronger than your situation. 'Cause your weakest moments are when you need to be at your strongest."

Lastly, Mike told William to call his wife and let her know that he'd be staying at his place tonight because they'd both been drinking and neither of them were in any condition to be driving.

William pulled out his cell phone and called his wife. They had a brief conversation, then he hung up the phone.

With his eyes Mike asked him, "What did she say?" William just shrugged his shoulders and shook his head depressingly in response.

At that time Mike looked at his friend and asked him, "Would you like for me to have Tabitha speak to Keisha? You know, see if she'll open up and tell her what's going on?"

For the first time that night William sat upright. And Mike saw an immediate happiness in his eyes as William quickly responded, "Yes, I think that would be a great idea!"

Leaning back on the sofa, Mike continued, "There's nothing at all that our wives don't talk about. Nothing's off limits between the two of them."

William replied, "I'm sure your wife Tabitha can get my wife Keisha to open up about what's causing her to shut down on me. I so desperately need to know. I'll try anything at this point to save my marriage," exclaimed William.

Acknowledging that the liquor that he'd consumed had him rambling on and on at this point, Mike decided to refocus his attention. So Mike jokingly mentioned that Tabitha might already be cognizant of what the underlying issues were.

Both guys immediately shared the same glance at one another. William pointed his finger at Mike and stated, "You just might be on to something. Is Tabitha home now?"

"Of course she is," responded Mike. "She's upstairs asleep. We'll sleep on things tonight and I'll speak with her about this in the morning," said Mike.

Both men shook hands in agreement. Mike told William, "You know where the guest bedroom is. Make yourself at home." And each of them went their separate paths for the night.

For the most part of the night, William laid in the guest bedroom restless, unable to fall asleep. Physically his body was tired. Yet his mind was running wildly with thoughts and reasons for his wife's unfavorable actions as of late.

Pulling out his cell phone, he began Googling complications during or after childbirth and the possible effects. And he surprisingly stumbled upon postpartum depression.

His mouth immediately fell open! As the symptoms that he was reading similarly related to the very issues he was currently experiencing at home with his wife.

In no time he grew thirsty for knowledge about postpartum depression. He found himself reading pages and pages about the condition.

William was clicking on site after site on his cell phone comparing notes, reviews and information. Gaining as much knowledge as he could on the topic.

It was well after 5 A.M. when he finally laid down and closed his eyes.

Around noon that day, William had woken up gotten himself together and was sitting at the kitchen table catching a bite to eat that had previously been prepared by Mike's wife Tabitha.

While William was eating, his good friend Mike walked into the kitchen, sat down and immediately asked him how he was feeling. William assured him that he felt much better.

Tabitha entered the kitchen and poured both guys a cup of coffee. She spoke for the first time, saying, "Seems you two were up drinking late again, this should help both of you." Both gentlemen thanked her and instantly took sips of their coffee.

Before Tabitha could exit the kitchen, her husband Mike stopped her asking her to sit and talk with them for a few. She nodded, agreed and took a seat at the table beside her husband.

Mike took a couple sips of his coffee, looked over at William, then asked his wife, "Hey, babe, have you talked to Keisha lately?"

Before responding, his wife got up and fixed herself a cup of coffee. Instead of sitting back down at the table beside her husband, she stood alongside the counter.

That noticeably puzzled William. He looked at Mike, then back to his wife before asking, "If you know anything, can you please help me?" Then he continued, "I'm fighting hard to save my marriage."

Tabitha walked over towards her husband, put her hand on his shoulder, took another sip of her coffee, then replied, "I deeply sympathize with you, William, and all that you're going through. I can only imagine the emotions and all that you've been enduring.

"However, the things that Keisha confided in me, I have to let those things remain between us. I mean that with all due respect to you. And I pray that you understand my position on this."

At that moment, William leaned back in his chair and looked at Mike before acknowledging to Tabitha that he did, in fact, understand. William stated that he didn't like it, yet he did understand and respected her loyalty to his wife.

His friend Mike pulled his wife Tabitha close to him and tried to convince her to spill a bean or two. Kissing her on her hand, her arm, her waist, her stomach, he asked, "Babe, can you just give him a general idea, please?"

Playfully Tabitha swayed her hips towards her husband's shoulders and asked, "Do I ask you to reveal anything to me that the two of you speak to one another about in confidence?" Mike gently rubbed his wife on the back, replying, "The little things that we talk about pale in comparison to something of this magnitude, babe."

Nodding her head in agreement, Tabitha folded her arms, stepped away from her husband and responded to him, saying, "Even though that might actually be true, whatever Keisha feels safe discussing with me will remain between the two of us."

Then she turned to William and said, "My heart is with you and your wife in what the two of you have been enduring. However, when she's ready to, I'm certain that she'll open up to you."

Even though it wasn't the answers that William was seeking, he thanked Tabitha for being a true friend to his wife. Tabitha nodded and began gathering the dishes off the table so that she could clean the kitchen.

A few seconds later, William was standing up and saying, "I believe it's time for me to be heading home." Mike stood up with his friend and said, "Come on, I'll walk you out."

On his way out, William stopped, turned and thanked Tabitha again. She nodded, then turned to start washing the dishes to hide the sudden wave of emotion that began to overwhelm her.

Out the corner of his eye, Mike noticed his wife's change in body language. William headed straight towards the front door and didn't notice at all. Mike took another look back at his wife before stepping outside of his front door with his friend. Something wasn't right within her and he immediately sensed it.

Both guys walked to William's car before either said anything. William spoke first, "Mike, I truly appreciate your efforts and continued loyalty on my behalf. Yet I believe this is a dilemma that I'll have to work out with my wife when she's ready to open up."

Even though Mike understood his good friend's reasoning, he had to alert him to what he personally thought could be the issue.

Reluctantly Mike said, "Hold, on Will, I've got some information that you might want to research." That stopped William from getting in his car.

With his hand he gestured to his friend to continue. Mike asked William, "Are you at all familiar with the term postpartum depression?" William smiled, then reached out and hugged his friend.

Stunned at William's reaction to his question, Mike asked, "Did I miss something? That big hug came out of nowhere."

"Not at all, my friend," William responded. Then he continued, saying, "I couldn't sleep last night. So I was scrolling on my cell phone, Googling possible conditions with or after pregnancy. And I came across postpartum depression. I was up until 5 or so reading and taking notes about the disorder."

That brought an innocent smile to Mike's face. "Now I see why you smiled and hugged me," replied Mike. Rubbing his chin, he continued, "They say if you want it bad enough that nothing will stop you from obtaining it. And we all know how much you love Keisha."

Staring off into the clouds, William responded to Mike, "Love is just another word when the action isn't present. Yes, I do love my wife. And I've been loyal and faithful in every aspect throughout our relationship. Yet I'm still a man. A man that has needs. Needs that are being neglected."

"Wait, wait, hold on," William exclaimed. "Mike! Don't get discouraged. And don't start giving in to temptation. You're stronger than this situation! That's not you!" Then Mike stepped back, looked William square in his eyes, and asked him, "Is this what you really want, Will?"

Shaking his head and shrugging his shoulders to implicate that he wasn't sure what he wanted right now, William got into his car and drove off. Mike stood there watching his friend drive away with a perturbed look on his face.

Chapter Eleven
Temptation

The moment that William pulled up at home, his attitude was different. He didn't have the same thought process as he did the day before. The pity, sorrow and empathy was presently absent within him.

As he approached his front door, he took a deep breath, then proceeded to enter.

Once inside there was complete silence. He walked in the kitchen, dining room, his daughter's bedroom, his son's bedroom, the master bedroom, and there wasn't a trace of anyone being home.

Standing in his bedroom for a few moments, William just stood there looking around at what had been him and his wife for years now.

He looked at the bed, which was neatly made and looked as if it hadn't even been slept in. His mind began to wander aimlessly at all of the times that he and his wife had made love in that very same bed.

There was a slight grin on his face for what seemed like seconds. The smile quickly faded as his thoughts were interrupted by the ringing of his cell phone. He pulled out his phone, glanced at the number that was calling and placed his phone back in his pocket.

Turning back to the bed before him, he attempted to recapture the moments that he was previously fantasizing about to no avail. The vibe just wasn't the same for him.

So he walked into the bathroom and just stared at the shower, their jacuzzi tub, the sink and even the huge rug that laid on the floor. These were all the places that William and his wife Keisha would be spontaneous and just go wildly at one another.

He stepped into the shower with all of his clothes on and just closed his eyes for what seemed like an eternity.

In his mind he was visualizing Keisha pleasuring him in the shower. She was kissing him softly on his neck, his chest and his abdomen. Before he could picture her going any lower, his cell phone rang again.

Not wanting his thoughts to be interrupted again, William didn't even pull out his cell phone to see who was calling him. He just let the call go to voicemail. He knew whoever was calling for him would leave a message if it was of any importance.

However, he was unable to continue with his fantasy because his cell phone immediately started ringing again.

Shaking his head in disbelief, William pulled out his cell phone to see who was calling him, yet he missed the call. He scrolled through his missed call log to learn that he had three missed calls from the same number. He didn't recognize the number offhand. And they didn't leave a message either.

That somewhat puzzled William. So he stood there for a while contemplating whether or not he should call the number back to see who it was that was trying to reach him.

After deciding not to, William stepped out of the shower and began to exit the bathroom.

On his way out of the bathroom, William caught a glimpse of himself in the mirror. And he hadn't really taken a look at himself in a while. He stopped and took a long look at himself.

He stood there proudly smiling as he realized that he was a very handsome man with a solid, square jaw line. His dark milk chocolate complexion was complemented nicely by some straight white teeth and a neatly trimmed full beard.

Licking his lips, he walked out of the bathroom and went to his drawer to get some clean underclothes. He fetched some clean towels and returned to the bathroom to take a shower.

Once William had taken all of his clothes off, he stood naked in front of the mirror. He noticed how well he had maintained his physique. William stood in the mirror flexing his pecs, abs and his biceps before saying to himself, "You don't let all this go to waste."

Clapping his hands loudly in approval, he stepped into the shower. William was no longer fantasizing now. He was excitedly singing love songs very loudly in the shower.

Remembering that he'd stayed out all night drinking and slept in the guest room at his friend's house, William decided to take a long shower.

After his shower he was putting on powder, deodorant, lotion and so forth when he suddenly heard his phone ringing. He walked over to his phone and saw that it was that same number calling him.

Staring at his cell phone, William briefly entertained the thought of answering his phone, then walked away from it, allowing it to go to voicemail again.

While brushing his teeth, he was thinking about the strange number calling him repeatedly. Then he shook it off and continued doing his hygiene and getting dressed.

Once fully dressed, William grabbed his keys, wallet and his cell phone. And before he made it out the door, his cell phone rang again. This time it was a number that he recognized. It was Mike calling to check up on him.

William assured Mike that he was good. Told him that he was going to get something to eat. Mike asked him where he was going. William stated that he was undecided. Mike responded where the two of them could go grab a bite to eat together and told his good friend William that he'd treat.

Of course, William wasn't going to object to a free lunch. And now that his friend Mike would be joining him, he wouldn't be alone either.

Knowing exactly where the establishment was, William didn't need to use his navigation. So he just turned his music on and let his thoughts roam as he drove.

William couldn't help but wonder if he should press Mike to put the pressure on his wife Tabitha for information about his wife Keisha. Yet he quickly dismissed the thought because he didn't want to possibly create friction and divide Mike and Tabitha within their home.

Unselfishly, William decided he'd just go with the flow of the conversation during lunch and not press the issue with Mike about his wife and what she knew.

Once William arrived at the restaurant, he was surprised that Mike had made it there before him. He walked in and Mike was waving him over to the table.

While walking over to the table to sit down with Mike for lunch, William noticed two very attractive ladies sitting at a table across from Mike.

Both of the ladies were flirting without saying a word. Mike looked in the direction of the ladies, then back to William and asked, "Are you trying to see if you still got it?" Both of the men laughed as William sat down at the table across from Mike.

The ladies continued flirting as the guys opened up their menus. Mike nudged William and motioned in the direction of the ladies.

For the first time both of the ladies waved to the guys. Mike smiled and signaled the ladies over to share a table with them.

Shocked at Mike's gesture, William leaned over to Mike and exclaimed, "We're both married men, what are you doing?" Mike whispered to William, "Are you telling me that you couldn't stand a little innocent female interaction?" William shot a blank expression at Mike. And Mike responded, "We're just eating lunch, Will, chill."

The waitress was coming over to take the guys' drink orders when the ladies joined both men at the table. Mike asked the ladies what they'd like to drink.

Not sure what they wanted to drink yet, Mike ordered waters for everyone, then he focused his immediate attention on the ladies that had joined them for lunch.

First Mike introduced himself to the ladies and told them what he did for a living. Then he introduced Will to the ladies and told them what he did for a living as well. William just simply nodded to both ladies and smiled.

The waitress came back quickly with their waters. Mike, noticing that William was somewhat uncomfortable, ordered a double Hennessy and Coke for William.

One of the ladies spoke up and ordered herself a vodka and cranberry juice. Her friend followed her lead and ordered herself a margarita. Mike smiled and said, "Now that we're all breaking the ice, make that two double Hennessy and Coke."

The waitress wrote down each of their orders, then reiterated them to Mike to make certain that she had each of their orders correct. Mike nodded that she in fact had their orders right. The waitress told her customers that she'd be right back with their drinks.

While they were waiting for the waitress to return with their drinks, Mike asked the ladies to tell them a little bit about themselves.

The first one to speak up introduced herself as Tiffany. She told the guys that she was a recently divorced mom of two teenagers in high school. She went on to state that love wasn't in her forecast. She married her husband young and hadn't experienced much outside of him. So she stated that she was just looking to open up and live a little.

Not one to let an opportunity go by, Mike chimed in, "So you're pretty much looking for friends with benefits type of situation, Ms. Tiffany. Am I correct?"

With no hesitation, Tiffany responded, "For the most part, yes, that's what I'm looking for right now." She continued, "I don't want to be tied down." She further stated, "I just want to feel alive and enjoy my life." Then she asked Mike, "Does that make sense to you?"

Nodding his head in agreement, Mike savagely responded, "Yes, that makes sense to me." Mike continued, "You're a grown woman that knows what she wants, looking to enjoy your life and not just live it according to the opinions of others."

Excitedly Tiffany replied, "Yes, that's exactly where I am in life." Then she continued, "I've been the good little faithful wife. And all that got me was lied to, cheated on and eventually divorced! I'm going to do me now," Tiffany said.

High-fiving Tiffany across the table, Mike replied, "I can totally respect that."

For the first time, Mike really took a long look at Tiffany. She was beautiful! Long jet-black hair hanging past her shoulders, caramel complexion, almond-shaped eyes, full luscious lips and a smile that could melt the coldest heart.

In his mind, Mike was thinking, *These are the women that guys be taking for granted, lying to and cheating on. Now she's another good woman gone bad.*

As Mike and Tiffany continued with their small talk, the other lady introduced herself to William as Stacy.

Before Stacy could reveal anything more than her name, the waitress returned to their table with their drinks. The waitress apologized for the delay. Mike said, "No problem at all. It actually gave all of us time to get better acquainted."

The waitress laughed, then asked, "Are you all ready to order now?" William finally spoke up and ordered his food first. He ordered a steak well done, loaded baked potato and steamed broccoli.

After writing William's order down, the waitress turned to Stacy and Tiffany, asking if they were ready to order. Tiffany ordered grilled shrimp and crab legs. Stacy looked at Tiffany and said, "That sounds like a winner to me, I'll have the same."

Turning her attention to Mike, the waitress asked, "And for you, sir?"

"I'll have the steak and lobster, steak well done with a side of scallops, please," replied Mike.

Once again the waitress repeated each order back to her customers to make sure that it was accurate. Each of them confirmed that their orders were correct.

Before the waitress could walk off, Mike asked Tiffany and Stacy if they would like some appetizers while they waited for their food. They both said yes. So Mike ordered some appetizers for each of them to devour as they small talked and waited for their orders.

Without hesitation, Mike asked Stacy, "So before the waitress came with our drinks, weren't you in the process of telling my good friend Will a little about you?" Mike winked at William. William returned a fake smile in Stacy's direction and a stern look in Mike's direction.

Stacy laughed and took a sip of her drink. You could easily tell that she was more conservative than her friend Tiffany. Stacy was a bit shy and reserved. Tiffany was definitely an extrovert at heart. As was Mike. That's probably why the two of them instantly hit it off. William was a better-looking guy than Mike. Yet what Mike lacked in looks he made up for in personality and he had money. So he never had a problem with the ladies.

Clean cut, nicely dressed, athletic built with a great smile was William. William had money as well. His personality was just more of an introvert. Well, until he had a few drinks in him. He'd certainly open up to the situation after consuming a few drinks. And William was taller than Mike as well.

Mike and William were business partners. Together they successfully ran their own business. Neither of them ever wanted to work for anyone else. So they went into business for themselves and became successful entrepreneurs.

Gaining some courage from a few sips of her drink, Stacy started telling William that she was single and free to mingle. She had a four-year-old son that she greatly adored. And her son was her life. She had very little free time for dating anyway 'cause she worked two jobs to hold down her household.

Feeling like she had been babbling and revealing too much, Stacy apologized for boring William about her poor little life.

To her surprise, William replied, "Your poor little life doesn't strike me as boring at all, Stacy." William continued, "I see an independent, devoted mother with gumption. That's both intriguing and commendable."

It had been awhile since Stacy received genuine compliments from a man that seemed as if he wasn't just trying to get her in bed. William's kind words fascinated Stacy. He seemed gentle, poised and mature. William spoke with a level of intelligence and didn't come across as a man that spoke just to hear himself talk. Stacy was looking William over and she thought to herself, *Damn, this is one fine man!*

Licking her lips, Stacy looked at William and said, "I've heard Mike mention a few things about you. Now how about you tell me some things about yourself, William."

Seizing the moment, Mike interrupted and said, "Excuse us for a second, please, ladies." Mike motioned with his head for William to follow him away from the table. Puzzled by Mike's sudden actions, William reluctantly got up and followed Mike outside to talk.

Soon as they both stepped outside, Mike said to William, "Do you see how fine that woman is? Stacy is finer than Tiffany and they're both beautiful women. I pulled you away from the table to make sure that you don't blow what potentially could be by talking about your marital problems," Mike just about mumbled to William. "The less she knows about you the better right now," Mike said to William.

"Say less," William responded to Mike. "You're not worried about Stacy 'cause you know me," William said to Mike. "And you know I'm not going to get involved with her," continued William. "You're worried about me blowing your opportunity to score with her friend Tiffany," William continued. "Don't worry, I won't be the spoiler," William told Mike.

While the guys were outside talking, the ladies were inside talking. Tiffany asked Stacy, "So what do you think?"

Stacy responded, "William is fine, girl, almost too fine!" Stacy continued speaking, "He's witty, intelligent, has his own money, you can tell he's not a man of many words and you can tell he's not just out to score."

Tiffany retorted, "Sounds like someone's crushing on William."

Both of the ladies erupted in laughter.

Channeling her focus to Tiffany, Stacy asked her, "Okay, what do you think about Mike?"

Tiffany replied, "He's smooth, a go-getter, a take-charge type of man, knows what he wants and I can tell that he's used to getting what he wants."

Stacy responded, "And by the way he was looking at you, I'd say that he wants you!"

Both ladies laughed out loud again. Then Tiffany replied, "I can see Mike being a possible friend with benefits." And the ladies shared another laugh.

Just as Mike and William were heading back to their table, the waitress, with assistance from a coworker, was setting their food on their table. As the gentlemen sat down, the waitress asked, "Will any of you be needing anything else at this time?"

Each person looked around at the other, then Mike assured her that they were good.

The waitress replied, "Well, my name is Tina if anyone needs anything." And the waitress walked off.

William bowed his head to bless his food. And he was slightly startled when he felt Stacy lock her hand in his. He opened his eyes and saw her smiling as she bowed her head with him. William went on to bless their food. They both said Amen when he finished. William found himself still holding Stacy's hand a few seconds after having blessed the food. He felt something that he couldn't explain.

It could be largely due to the fact that he hadn't touched a woman nor been touched by a woman in a year with all that had been transpiring with his wife. Regardless of what it was, William felt a wave of excitement. And he was thinking about that while he ate his food.

The other two just bowed their heads while William was blessing the food. Then Mike and Tiffany began eating and talking.

There was plenty of small talk going around the table as each one of them were enjoying their meals. Tiffany started asking William questions. And he engaged her for the most part. Mike began asking Stacy questions as well. And to Mike's surprise, not only did Stacy answer his questions, she had some questions of her own.

By now each of their drinks had kicked in and everyone was a bit more talkative.

Of course, Mike knew that the double Hennessy with Coke would open William up. So he was keeping a close ear to William's conversation as well. Making sure that he didn't get a loose tongue and slip up.

However, it did help the little lunch rendezvous go a lot smoother. William was fully engaged at the table now. As he was telling stories and cracking jokes, Stacy was laughing at each of William's punchlines, too. She really seemed to get his humor.

Several times after William told a joke, Stacy patted his thigh while laughing. That aroused William beyond Stacy's recognition. She even squeezed his inner thigh a couple of times and her nails gingerly stroked his flesh. Stacy went exploring without being obvious with her intentions. And she found out exactly what she was hoping. William was definitely her kind of man.

Noticing the vibe between Stacy and William, Mike signaled the waitress over and ordered another round of drinks for each of them. Mike already knew that he was scoring with Tiffany. Now he wanted to get his friend William to come all the way out of his loyal husband phase, forget about all of his problems at home with his wife and enjoy a great time with the beautiful woman practically sitting in his lap right now.

Once Mike ordered another round of drinks, Tiffany slid her chair closer to his and whispered in his ear, "Are you trying to get me drunk?"

Mike charmingly responded, "Not drunk, just in the mood." Then he squeezed her inner thigh and winked at her.

Without question, Mike was definitely a charmer at heart. Unlike his friend William, Mike wasn't at all faithful to his wife. He was known to use his wit, charisma and money to sleep around with various women outside of his marriage. And right now he had Tiffany eating out of the palm of his hand by playing the "money isn't a thing" role. Because Tiffany was attracted to men that had money, power and status.

The waitress returned with the round of drinks that Mike had just ordered. She handed each person their drink and took their empty glasses from their previous drinks.

"Will there be anything else, dessert, coffee or tea?" asked the waitress.

Immediately Mike surveyed the table, anticipating a response from someone at the table, they all nodded that they were okay. The waitress acknowledged their responses and proceeded to the kitchen area with their empty glasses.

Raising his glass to propose a toast, Mike said to the group, "Please raise your glasses with me." Each of them raised their glasses to the center of the table. Then Mike said, "To laughter, great food and the good time that we've all enjoyed together today." They all toasted and took sips of their drinks.

Letting out a huge sigh after sipping her drink, Stacy laid her head on William's shoulder and patted her hand on his chest. The very moment that William turned his head in her direction, the scent of Stacy's perfume intoxicated his senses. William took another sip of his drink and relaxed in his chair.

Trying to fight back what he was feeling, William found himself getting turned on by Stacy's scent and her touch. He hadn't smelled a woman nor been touched by a woman in over a year now. And the fact that he'd been drinking Hennessy didn't make it any easier for him.

Tapping Stacy on her shoulder, William excused himself from the table, saying that he needed to use the restroom. Stacy spoke up and said, "I need to use the little girls' room myself."

Tiffany excused herself as well and said, "I'll come with you."

Mike was the only one that remained at the table.

Seeing just about everyone fleeing the table, the waitress walked over and asked Mike if he would be needing anything else. Mike thanked her for her service and told her she could bring him the check. The waitress asked Mike, "Will this all be on one check?"

Mike replied, "Yes."

The waitress smiled and told Mike that she'd be right back with the check.

As the waitress walked off from the table, Mike was watching her walk from behind. He said to himself, "Tina has potential." Mike sat there hoping that Tina returned with the check before Tiffany and Stacy returned to the table. He had that look in his eye. Mike was set to try to conquer.

To Mike's amazement, William returned to the table first. And Mike wasted no time filling William in on his new discovery with the waitress, Tina. William shook his head and said, "Mike, you really should slow down with all of these women."

"Slow down!" Mike exclaimed. "Hold that thought, she's coming with the check," Mike told William.

The waitress approached the table with the check and Mike asked her, "Excuse me, Tina, are you old enough to drink, dance and have a good time with a complete gentleman?"

Tina responded, "Are you asking me on a date?"

Mike replied, "Yes, I am." Then he pulled out his cell phone and asked her for her phone number.

Tina asked Mike, "What about the lady you're here on this lunch date with?"

Mike replied, "I saw two ladies dining alone, so I invited them to dine with me and my business partner."

Tina looked at William, then looked at Mike side-eyed, yet she gave him her phone number anyway.

Just as Mike was saving Tina's phone number, Tiffany and Stacy were coming back to the table. Mike handed Tina his card to take care of the payment for the food.

Tina said, "I'll be right back with your receipt."

Both Tiffany and Stacy sat down at the table. Tiffany spoke first, saying, "I'm going to take the rest of my food to go."

Stacy replied, "Me too."

Mike spoke up, "I'll have the waitress bring us all some to-go boxes. It seems we all drank more than we ate," continued Mike.

They all shared a brief laugh together. Then Mike looked at Tiffany and asked her, "So what are your plans for the rest of the day?"

Tiffany licked her lips, then responded, "I can be free if I need to be. How about you, Mr. Mike?" asked Tiffany.

"I have some paperwork to go over with William this afternoon," Mike replied. "However, give me your number and I'll call you after we're done," said Mike.

Tiffany obliged Mike and gave him her number.

Looking at Stacy, Tiffany gestured with her head for her to say something to William. Stacy nervously shook her head no to her friend Tiffany. Because she felt William should make the move and not her.

Not one to miss an opportunity, Mike picked up on the energy between Tiffany and Stacy. So he took it upon himself to speak up and tell William and Stacy they should exchange numbers and keep in touch as well.

Mike also said to William and Stacy, "I know I'm not the only person at this table that has witnessed the chemistry between the two of you."

Tiffany cleared her throat and said, "I've witnessed the animal attraction over there." Then she winked at her friend Stacy.

With little to no thought about what he was doing, William asked Stacy for her number. Stacy smiled big, bright and pretty at William and gave him her number. William looked at Stacy and asked, "You don't have much free time working two jobs and tending to your son, though, right?"

Stacy responded, "I work a full-time job during the week and a part-time job on the weekends." Then Stacy continued talking to William, saying, "But I have no problem making time for you, though."

That instantly brought a smile to William's face. To hear an attractive woman say that she'd make time for him made William feel good.

He'd been longing for this type of attention from his wife, to smell her again, touch her again, and he'd experienced all of what he wasn't receiving at home from his wife in less than an hour with this beautiful stranger sitting next to him in this expensive restaurant.

The thoughts that were going through William's mind at the moment as he was now face to face with Stacy. His mind was flirting with all the things that he knew he shouldn't be thinking as a married man.

In a split second his thoughts were interrupted by the waitress bringing Mike's credit card back to the table. Tina said to the group, "I hope each one of you enjoyed your food and drinks. It was a pleasure serving you today," Tina continued.

Before Tina could walk away from the table, Mike pulled out a crisp fifty-dollar bill and handed it to Tina. "Thank you for all of your great service today," Mike said to Tina.

"Excitedly, Tina said, "Thank you!" She put the money in her apron and began clearing their table.

Now that they were all standing up to leave the restaurant, William was able to get a better view of Stacy's figure. She was well put together. Nicely proportioned. Full, inviting breasts that looked like they sat up without assistance from her bra, slim waist, flat stomach with curvaceous hips, nice round, firm butt that had William intrigued and nicely toned legs. William could tell that she worked out. Her body was fit yet very sexy.

"Are you going to stare at her or take a picture?" Mike joked to William.

Everyone laughed except William. He didn't notice that he'd zoned out and was openly staring at Stacy. William instantly felt slightly embarrassed.

Stacy walked over to William and whispered in his ear, "Don't be embarrassed. I've been looking you over since the moment you first walked your fine self into this restaurant."

William cracked a smile and began walking Stacy to her car.

Once they were all outside, Mike gave Tiffany a hug and assured her that he'd see her later. She smiled at him and said, "Don't stand me up." Tiffany waved to her friend Stacy, then she got in her car.

William walked Stacy to her car and opened her car door for her.

"Oh, and you're a gentleman," Stacy said to William. "You're too fine, too smooth and too kind to be single," Stacy said to William.

William laughed and responded, "You're pouring it on thick."

Stacy pressed her body to William's and said, "Thick like cold peanut butter!"

William laughed again.

The two of them finally embraced and hugged one another. William felt the warmth from Stacy's body heat and smelled the fragrance from her perfume again. William closed his eyes while holding Stacy and just allowed the smell of this beautiful woman to overwhelm him for a few seconds.

When he opened his eyes and they both were disengaging from their lengthy embrace, Stacy kissed him softly on his cheek. She got into her car and said to William, "I hope to hear from you soon." William smiled and Stacy pulled off.

By the time William had made it to his car, Mike had pulled his car next to William's. Mike looked William square in his eye and said to him, "You better not let that beautiful woman down." Then he pulled off before William could respond.

William stood there for a few moments reflecting on what had just taken place. *You're a married man,* he said to himself. His thoughts just continued to wander, *You're an honest man, you're not a cheater, you've never cheated on your wife, don't start now,* he thought. Then he looked at his finger and realized that he wasn't even wearing his ring! What had he just allowed himself to get into? He started his truck and drove the long route back to his house, allowing himself time to think and clear his head.

Chapter Twelve
The Bridge

While pulling up to his house and parking in his driveway, William noticed that his wife's car still wasn't home. He didn't think much of it. It was still early in the day. She could've been out running errands, over her mother or sister's house or out having a fun day with the kids.

Either way it was alright with William. Because it gave him time to sit down, reflect and sort out his thoughts. It was strange to him that he was even contemplating communicating with Stacy ever again. Yet he couldn't stop thinking about how beautiful Stacy was. She was gorgeous, actually! He could still smell her sweet perfume and feel her tender touch.

Walking into his house, William decided that he needed to shower again to get Stacy's scent off of him. He took his shirt off and could smell Stacy's perfume all over it. Fumbling with the dirty clothes hamper, William decided he'd wash a load of clothes to prevent the scent from lingering in the dirty clothes basket for his wife to discover later.

After throwing a load of clothes in the washing machine, William walked into the bathroom and turned the shower on.

While in the shower, William tried to think about his wife and how he was going to approach her about postpartum depression. He knew it wasn't going to be easy to get Keisha to open up.

The more that William tried to focus on how he was going to break through to Keisha, the more his thoughts reflected back to Stacy. William stepped directly under the shower head and allowed the water to run over his head in an attempt to clear his thoughts.

After minutes of letting the hot water pour over his head, William began to shower and just let his thoughts run wildly.

It seemed like the more William tried to focus on what he needed to do to work on his failing marriage, the more he kept thinking about the fun in the sun that he could be enjoying with Stacy. William thought about the way he felt when Stacy touched him, the effect that the scent of her perfume had on him and how she fondled him under the table and knew that he had a major erection!

There was no escaping his thoughts. No matter how many times William closed his eyes and tried to think about something else, his thought process was right back to Stacy. As William was drying off, he started imagining how soft Stacy's nicely toned body was, how smooth her delicate skin was and how kissable her full lips were.

Aside from the fact that Stacy was as gorgeous as she was, William was vastly growing to be fascinated with the peculiar idea of having an affair with a stranger.

With no regards to anything else around him, William stood facing his bathroom mirror donning nothing but the bath towel that he'd just dried off with. His muscular chest, shoulders and chiseled biceps were glistening before him, complemented by his six-pack abs. William thought out loud to himself there once was a time that he could just take his shirt off and his wife Keisha would be all over him.

Lately William was starting to feel like he was living with a stranger. Keisha no longer responded to any of his advances, didn't want William to touch her, slept with pillows between them in the bed, and it seemed to William that Keisha was making it a point to not be home alone with him. The fire was gone in their marriage. The smoke had all but settled.

Yet William still loved his wife. And he didn't want to leave his wife or tear his family apart. So divorce wasn't an option for him at this time. However, he had physical needs that his wife had completely turned a blind eye to.

Up until this point in their marriage, William had never even thought about breaking his vows. He knew how often his friend Mike had affairs on his wife Tabitha. Yet William never entertained the thought of cheating on his wife Keisha.

Often William wondered if Tabitha knew that Mike was cheating and having random affairs on her. The fact that he took care of home and never brought his dirt where they laid their heads together, did that make her allow it, not acknowledge it or did she not care because the other women were doing what she didn't want to do sometimes?

Either way, situations like this now had William thinking outside of the box for once in his young adult life. Is this a situation or a secret arrangement that could actually work within his home since his wife had no desire to please him in any way? Is it considered cheating if your wife knows about it and she's alright with it?

At that moment, William decided that he was going to talk to his friend Mike about some of the things that had just run through his mind. He had no doubt that Mike would give him the profound answers that he needed in the midst of all of these puzzling questions that he'd recently stumbled upon.

Heading into his bedroom, William went to his dresser, then his closet in search of the appropriate attire to put on for the remainder of the day. After laying an outfit and some shoes out onto his bed, William went into the bathroom and gathered his body spray, cologne, lotion, baby powder and deodorant.

Once William located his Bluetooth speaker, he turned some music on. He was vibing to each song that came on as he put powder under each arm, then applied his deodorant. Then he began putting lotion on his body. He started with his face and neck, all the way down to his legs and feet. William sprayed his body spray on his bare chest and abdomen. Then he proceeded to put his clothes on.

Fully dressed, William looked himself over in the mirror and was satisfied with the clothes that he had opted to wear. He put some cologne on, grabbed his phone, his keys and headed downstairs to get in his truck.

Before he started his truck, he called Mike on the phone to find out where he was. Mike told William that he was in the office going over some paperwork. William responded that he was on his way into the office and he needed to talk to him. Mike replied, "I'll see you when you get here."

Once William hung up the phone, he ran back into his house to retrieve his briefcase. His phone rang twice, then it stopped. So he didn't bother to reach in his pocket to see who was calling him. William was walking out of his door and his phone started ringing again.

This time he set his briefcase down and pulled his phone out to answer it. The phone number looked familiar to William, yet he wasn't sure who it was. So he didn't answer it. He put his cell phone back in his pocket, picked up his briefcase and got into his truck.

To William's surprise, his wife Keisha was pulling up to their house as he was backing out of the driveway. William backed out of the driveway and allowed his wife to pull into the driveway. Then he pulled back into the driveway and parked his truck behind her.

Through the tinted windows on her Benz, William didn't notice that his kids weren't in the car with Keisha. She was just sitting in her car. So William got out of his truck and walked up to his wife's car window. He stood there for a minute or so before she even slightly cracked her window.

Bothered by his wife's nonchalant attitude, William sternly said to his wife, "Keisha, we need to talk and I mean now!"

Keisha rolled her window down a little further and replied to William, "Start talking, I'm listening."

William took a step back, looked up to the sky, then said to his wife, "So I'm supposed to talk to my wife through a partially rolled-down tinted window?"

Keisha rolled her window all the way down and sat there with her arms folded, looking in the opposite direction that her husband was standing, then said, "Is that better?"

Laughing it off, William looked at his wife sitting annoyingly before him and responded, "Don't even worry about it, Keisha." This is the last day, last time, last moment that I'll accept this treatment from you. I've done nothing but love you, be there for you and I've never broken our vows." William continued, "You treat me like I hurt you, had an affair on you or something."

The whole time that William was talking, Keisha just sat there unresponsive, scrolling on her cell phone. William laughed again and told Keisha, "I'm done wasting my breath, my time and my energy with this. For more than a year now, you've shown me that you don't care how I feel, what I want, what I need or nothing," William continued. "Point well taken, my love," William told his wife. "Don't wait up for me," William said to his wife as he turned and began walking back to his truck.

While walking to his truck, Keisha was looking at William through her rearview mirror. She rolled her window up, turned her car off and got out of her car. She stood there watching William back out of the driveway. Keisha wanted to stop William from leaving, yet she just stood there and watched him pull off.

Beyond upset at the time, William didn't even look in his mirror to see that his wife was standing in the driveway crying, watching him pull off.

Instead William pulled out his cell phone and scrolled to Stacy's number. He looked at her number and thought about calling her. Yet he set his phone down and decided not to. He turned the radio up in his truck and zoned out while he drove to the offices where he and Mike ran their business.

The music was so loud in William's truck that he didn't notice that his wife had called him several times while he was driving. He didn't notice that Keisha had called him until he pulled up and parked in his reserved parking spot outside of his office.

Turning his music down and turning his truck off, William grabbed his phone and saw the missed calls from his wife. He looked at his phone and thought about not calling her back. But that just wasn't the type of man that William was.

So he pressed the talk button and called his wife back. She didn't answer. So he called her again. The phone rang and rang and still Keisha didn't answer. So William threw his phone in his briefcase, grabbed his briefcase, chirped the alarm on his truck and walked toward his place of business.

Somewhat frustrated at this point, William went straight to his office and set his briefcase down on his desk. He flopped his tense body down on the chair behind his desk and started fumbling with the massage controls on the remote.

Walking by her boss's office and noticing that he had just come in, his assistant Sherrie peeked her head into his office and asked William, "Boss, will you be needing me for anything this afternoon?"

"Can you please bring me a bottle of water and some ibuprofen?" William asked his assistant.

"Sure thing, boss, be right back," commented Sherrie.

No sooner than Sherrie left William's office to go and retrieve the bottle of water and the ibuprofen that he requested, William's phone was ringing and vibrating in his briefcase. He sat up, opened his briefcase and pulled his phone out. It had stopped ringing by the time he attempted to answer it. He checked his missed call log and noticed it was the same mysterious number that had been trying to call him earlier that day.

A bit puzzled yet partly curious, William sat there contemplating calling the number back to see who it was that was continuously trying to reach him throughout the day. He knew it wasn't about business. Because the person was calling his personal cell phone.

Before he could make a sound decision, his phone rang again. It was his wife calling again. William decided not to take her call. He pressed ignore and sent her to his voicemail.

Although William wanted to know what his wife wanted, he didn't bother to answer his phone. Instead he reclined back in his chair, closed his eyes and reflected on how awful his wife had been to him over the past year.

Having fallen deep into his thoughts, William didn't realize that his assistant had returned with his bottle of water and his ibuprofen. Sherrie cleared her throat a couple of times to alarm William of her presence.

Sherrie sat the bottle of water and ibuprofen on William's desk, then asked, "Is everything alright, boss?"

"Just a slight headache," William responded.

Sherrie walked around behind William's chair and said, "Here, let me give you a massage and help you relax."

William replied, "That would be greatly appreciated, you always take good care of me, Sherrie. What would I do without you?" asked William.

Spinning his chair around so that he was face to face with her, Sherrie leaned in close to William and asked, "Do you want me to honestly answer that question?"

William looked Sherrie square in her eyes and replied, "Honesty has always been the best policy."

Sitting down before William on top of his desk, Sherrie began telling William how approximately one year ago, she noticed a change in his demeanor. She continued, "Your walk has been different, your conversations have been short with everyone around the office, you don't smile anymore and you always look tense or unhappy."

Flashing a slight grin, William asked, "Is there anything that you haven't noticed?"

Sherrie opened her legs in front of William while still sitting on his desk and said, "I know that you really love your wife when you've had all of this walking around you daily and you haven't even attempted to sample it."

Noticing that Sherrie wasn't wearing any undergarments somewhat aroused William. Yet he didn't let her know that he was turned on. He shrugged his shoulders and asked Sherrie, "How about finishing that massage?"

Stepping down off of William's desk and going back behind his chair to continue giving him a massage, Sherrie said, "Precisely my point. I won't utter another word about it," continued Sherrie.

William tried to relax in the chair and not think about Sherrie making a pass at him. Yet the tender touch of her fingers and the sensation stemming from it was stimulating his erotic senses.

The manner in which his body began to relax, Sherrie knew she was beginning to have an effect on William. He had the slightest clue how long Sherrie had been fantasizing about having an affair with her boss. She went from his broad shoulders and neck area down to his well-defined chest. Sherrie playfully ran her finely manicured fingernails across William's chest. The more Sherrie playfully caressed William, the more she felt him relax.

Totally relaxed by now, head back, eyes closed, William was thoroughly enjoying the feel of Sherrie's hands all over his upper body.

His moment was abruptly interrupted when Mike walked into his office and asked, "Sherrie, can you come to my office and thoroughly rub me down next? I'm feeling a little tension in my neck and shoulders, too," chuckled Mike.

William quickly straightened up and said, "Thank you, Sherrie. I'm feeling much better now," continued William.

Sherrie looked at Mike and said, "You have enough traffic in and out of your office, Mister Man."

Then she smiled, looked at William and said, "Page me if you need me, boss."

William nodded, stood up and saw Sherrie out.

After closing the door, William turned around to sit down and talk to Mike. "I see you're learning the ropes fairly quickly," Mike joked to William.

"Sherrie noticed that I was tensed and was simply giving me a massage," William replied sarcastically to Mike.

Nodding his head, Mike replied, "She's never offered to give me a massage."

"That's because she knows you have bad intentions, Mike," said William.

They both shared a quick laugh. Then their laughter was interrupted when Keisha walked into William's office. She spoke to Mike. Then asked him if he could give her a few minutes to talk to her husband. Mike nodded and got up to leave, yet William said, "No, he doesn't need to leave, Keisha, you do."

Both Mike and Keisha looked at William with shocked expressions on their faces.

Keisha, fighting through her tears, yelled at William, "How dare you?"

William replied, "How dare you, Keisha? Now that you finally want to talk, I'm supposed to just stop everything that I'm doing and listen?"

Keisha cut William off, saying, "It took everything in me to drive here to talk to you."

Choked up from her tears and emotions, Keisha flopped herself down in a chair and began sobbing frantically.

Mike said, "I'm going to leave the two of you to talk." He walked out and closed the door behind him.

Chapter Thirteen
Stubborn Love

Normally William would bolster his wife in times like this. Keisha knew that her husband didn't like to see her cry. And he promised her that he'd never be the reason that she cried. So his adamant behavior at the moment was baffling to her.

After moments of sitting in a chair across the desk from her husband sobbing uncontrollably, Keisha tried to pull herself together and communicate with William. She reached on top of his desk to grab a box of Kleenex. Keisha dried her face and blew her nose several times.

All the while that Keisha was having her meltdown, William was buried in the paperwork that was on his desk. As if his wife wasn't sitting a foot or so in front of him crying her eyes out. William showed no emotion nor concern for his wife.

Between her sniffles, Keisha began asking her husband questions. Her emotions intensified with each question that she asked him.

"William, what has gotten into you? Why are you treating me like this? When did you stop caring? Who is she, William, huh? Who is she? Are you cheating on me?" Keisha stood up, slammed both of her palms on William's desk and yelled, "Answer me, dammit!"

Raising his head to finally acknowledge his wife standing before him dramatically in a wave of emotion, William leaned back in his office chair and calmly spoke to his wife, saying, "The nerve of you, Keisha. To barge into my place of business asking me questions based on your own insecurities, assuming that I've been unfaithful and demanding answers from me," continued William.

Standing up, William continued talking to his wife, saying, "I'm the same man that was just trying to talk to his wife in our driveway and she totally gave me her rear end to kiss. The same man that has been trying to communicate with his wife, tried to seek counseling with his wife and been there for his wife in every way that a husband should."

Pacing the floor, William continued, "Keisha, I'm your husband and you're my wife! We don't even talk! You've been given me the silent treatment for a whole year now! You haven't had more than a few words to say to me and I still come home every day! We haven't been physical since Jr. was born. You haven't touched me, kissed me, hugged me, nothing of the sort!"

Suddenly William stopped pacing, looked directly at his wife, then said, "You even sleep with clothes on and put pillows between us in the bed, Keisha!"

Dropping her head, Keisha sat down in a chair on the opposite side of the desk from her husband. Keisha tried to respond and was interrupted by William.

"No, Keisha, you've said more than enough with your silence and with your little outburst here. It's about time that you listen and hear me out," said William.

Setting her purse on her husband's desk, Keisha sat back in the chair prepared to hear her husband out. William sat back down in his chair behind his desk so he wouldn't be standing over his wife while talking to her.

"The moment that we started dating, I knew you were the woman that I wanted to spend the rest of my life with. My spirit connected with yours. We miraculously fed off of one another's energy. There was no doubt in my mind that I wanted you to be my wife," said William.

Again Keisha tried to say something and William replied, "No, Keisha, let me finish. I stepped up in every way that a man is supposed to for the woman that he loves. I've been there for you and not once turned my back on you. No matter what we were going through, I've stood faithfully by your side. Not once have I ever broken our vows! Not once!" William reiterated.

Their conversation was interrupted by William's cell phone ringing loudly. He picked it up and looked at the number that was calling him. It looked familiar, yet he didn't recognize it. So he didn't answer the call.

Looking at his wife, William asked her, "Where was I?"

She replied, "You were saying that you've never broken our vows. And I appreciate that, William," Keisha said.

Holding up one finger, William said, "Hold on, I'll hear you out entirely, Keisha. Just let me get some things off of my chest first."

Keisha, being a submissive wife, obliged her husband by allowing him to continue on with what he needed to divulge to her. Keisha nodded and replied, "Go ahead, William, I'm listening."

Then he asked his wife, "Why has it taken you a whole year to want to talk to me, share a space with me, not to mention show any emotion? You care now? You're concerned now? Oh, did you remember that you have a husband now? Where's all of these tears coming from, all of a sudden?" William continued saying, "You haven't pleasured me in any way in over a year. I'm a man, I have needs, Keisha!

"You've walked past me in our own house for months and didn't even look at me! I'd walk into a room in our house and you'd get up and go to another room. I've come home from long days at this office praying that this would be the night that things were back to normal.

Only to come home to no dinner and continued silent treatment from you," William said to Keisha.

"Everyone has their breaking point, Keisha. And today in our driveway, I finally reached mine," William said. "I refuse to spend one more night enduring any more of this sheer unfairness from you when I've been a completely devoted, faithful husband to you.

"It's obvious that you stopped caring and gave up on us some time ago. Well, today I've decided to stop caring and give up, too. I need and deserve the same love, honor and respect in return from my wife that I'm giving her," William told Keisha.

"Relationships are give and take. So give your all to your significant other and take nothing about them for granted. You've taken me for granted and given me no reason to continue on with this broken marriage for far too long now, Keisha," William said.

"So I've decided to move out and let you keep the house with the kids," William continued saying. Then he took off his wedding ring, set it on the desk in front of his wife and said, "I'm also filing for divorce, Keisha. We haven't been consistently functioning in this relationship in over a year now and I don't foresee that changing," said William.

Then William sat back in his chair and told his wife that he'd said everything that he needed to. "You have the floor now, Keisha, I'm listening," William said to his wife.

By now Keisha was unable to control her emotions. She broke down crying heavily in front of William. There were no words coming from Keisha, just a very loud, deep, emotional cry. Keisha was sitting at William's desk with her head down bawling her eyes out!

There was a knock at the door and before William could get to the door to see who it was, his assistant Sherrie was walking in asking, "Boss, is everything alright in here?"

"Everything is fine, just having a conversation with Keisha," William said.

Dismissing William's lack of respect for his wife by acknowledging her by her name and not as his wife, Sherrie put her hand on Keisha's back and asked her, "Are you alright, Mrs. Jones?"

Keisha was still sobbing uncontrollably at the time. Therefore unable to respond to Sherrie. So Sherrie pulled a chair next to Keisha and continued to rub Keisha's back.

While Sherrie was attempting to console William's wife, he had sat back down in his chair, going over paperwork as if he had absolutely no concern about his wife's current condition.

After a few minutes had gone by, Sherrie looked over at William and asked him, "So you're really sitting there worrying about work opposed to the health and concern of your wife? She's certainly going through something right now. And she needs you," Sherrie continued.

The fact that William completely ignored Sherrie and showed no empathy whatsoever for his wife made Sherrie raise her voice and yell at William, "You are a distasteful man if you really sit there and witness the condition your wife is in and you do nothing to remedy the situation!"

William shot a stern look in Sherrie's direction and continued reading over the papers in front of him.

"So you're really just going to sit there and do nothing?" asked Sherrie. "Is this how you treat your wife?" asked Sherrie. "I've always thought so highly of you, William," Sherrie continued. "You're really not a good person at all," said Sherrie. "No real man would stubbornly sit there and allow his wife to cry like this," Sherrie told William.

Once again, William looked at Sherrie with an extremely displeasing look on his face, yet he didn't utter a word in response to all of the questions she was blurting out at him.

Shaking her head in sheer disbelief at William, still rubbing Keisha's back, Sherrie asked Keisha if she could get her something to drink. Keisha nodded her head no. Sherrie got up and excused herself to go and get her a bottle of water anyway.

The moment that Sherrie exited the room, Keisha raised up and tried to say something to William, then she just collapsed on the floor in front of him. William ran over to the other side of his desk, bent down and was calling Keisha's name. He checked her pulse and didn't get one.

Beginning to panic, William decided to check and see if Keisha was breathing. She wasn't breathing either! So he quickly began performing CPR on Keisha.

Just as William was attempting to revive Keisha, Sherrie walked back into the room with a bottle of water and a towel. She immediately dropped the bottle of water, fell to her knees alongside Keisha and yelled at William, "What did you do to her?" Sherrie started punching and slapping William wildly, steadily yelling, "What did you do to her, what did you do?"

All of the noise from the commotion caused Mike to come walking into William's office. Closing the door behind him, he asked, "What's going on in here, we can clearly hear you guys down the hall?" Once he saw Keisha laying on the floor unresponsive, he pried Sherrie off of William.

Now William was able to focus on trying to breathe life back into his wife. However, after continuing to fail, Sherrie told both William and Mike to move, saying she had her certification for CPR.

With Sherrie now performing CPR on Keisha, William was able to enlighten Mike on how Keisha passed out. That was also Sherrie's first time hearing how Keisha passed out after she had just left the room.

Mike asked William, "Did you call 911?"

William replied, "No, it just happened."

Mike told William, "Give me your phone."

William handed Mike his phone and Mike called 911 to alert the proper authorities to send help asap.

Just as Mike was hanging up from the 911 call, William's phone rang. Without thinking, Mike answered William's phone, saying, "Hello, hello, uh, hello." No one responded. So he disconnected the call and handed William his phone back.

Setting his phone on the desk, William quickly returned his focus to his wife Keisha, who was lying on the office floor before him unconscious, not breathing and with no pulse.

There was some small talk being exchanged between William and Mike about Keisha and the events leading up to her current dilemma until Sherrie nervously said, "Guys, I think we've lost her."

A huge roar erupted from deep inside of William as he dropped to his knees and yelled out loudly, "NNNNNOOOOOOOOOOO!!!!!!"

Both Sherrie and Mike attempted to offer support to William as he began calling out to God, "Please don't take my wife, Father, I apologize for the things I said, I love her, I promise I'll do right by her and please give me one more chance to love her in a way that'll be pleasing in your eyes, Father."

By now several people had gathered right outside of William's office as his loud roar had sparked curiosity in some of his employees working down the hall from him. They were whispering and pointing towards his office.

One of the older female employees approached his office door. She knocked a couple times and opened the door. Instantly she saw William hugging a lifeless form of his wife on the floor with Sherrie and Mike standing nearby. She ran into his office asking, "Did anyone call for help?"

Mike quickly responded, "Yes, I called 911 and help is on the way."

With William's office door opened now, other employees had gathered around outside and were standing there with their hands over their mouths in shock at the sight of what they were witnessing.

Amidst all of the sudden commotion outside of William's office, the paramedics were making their way down the hallway. The sounds of their radios alarmed Sherrie, Mike, William and the older lady Ms. Johnson that help was imminently approaching.

People standing in the hallway outside of William's office began to clear a path for the paramedics to gain entrance inside of William's office. Sherrie, Mike and Ms. Johnson each stepped out into the hallway, leaving only William inside of his office with the ambulance crew.

One of the paramedics began asking William a series of questions as two others were working diligently on reviving Keisha. The first time the medics used the defibrillator it made Keisha's body jump violently, causing William to turn his head because he couldn't bear to watch his wife in that state. The medic yelled out, "Clear," then shocked Keisha's body again. And again her body jumped violently in response to the equipment being utilized to regain her consciousness.

Almost in tears now, William asked the medic that had been questioning him, "Please, is there another way to do this? Is there anything less painful that you guys can do?"

Each time that William witnessed his wife's body elevate off the floor, it was ripping him apart inside. He thought the EMTs were adding insult to injury and hurting his wife more. William didn't want his wife to suffer. He vehemently pounded his fist against his office wall several times while sorrowfully fighting back tears.

Both Sherrie and Mike stepped in to calmly remove William from his office to prevent him from further disrupting the paramedics from performing their given duties.

The EMT positioned Keisha's body so they could roll her onto the stretcher. Once they had her body safely secured on the stretcher, one of the medics continued working on Keisha as the other two began rolling her body out of William's office and toward outside to insert her into the ambulance.

Walking stride for stride with the paramedics was William. He wasted no time getting into the back of the ambulance so that he could ride to the hospital with his wife. William held Keisha's hand and started praying as the ambulance began to take off.

Suddenly William felt Keisha squeeze his hand and he excitedly alerted one of the medics thinking that she was alright. Then the medic crushed William's hopes by saying, "That reaction could've been caused by her nervous system."

Following the ambulance at a safe distance was Mike. Sherrie had gotten into the truck with Mike. Noticing the severity of the situation, Mike pulled out his cell phone and called his wife to alert her on what had taken place and where they were headed. She assured him that she'd meet them there.

A phone began ringing inside of Mike's truck. He looked at Sherrie and she shrugged, saying, "That isn't my phone ringing." Then Mike chuckled as he remembered that he had grabbed William's cell phone off his desk for him. Yet by the time Mike had reached in his jacket pocket to retrieve William's phone, it had already stopped ringing.

Therefore, he didn't check the number to see who had called. Mike just slid the phone back in his pocket. He figured he'd let William check his own phone.

Meanwhile in the back of the ambulance, Keisha laid motionless with William unable to take his eyes off of his wife. He prayed to God that their marriage wouldn't end like this.

Chapter Fourteen
Regrets

Once the ambulance arrived at the hospital, the EMTs were rushing to get Keisha inside of the hospital. William followed close behind, then he had to take a seat in the waiting room. William couldn't stay seated for long. He was up pacing back and forth at the desk, asking questions and thinking every time the sliding doors opened that it was the doctor coming to talk to him.

The first to greet and support William at the hospital was Sherrie. Soon as she spotted him standing close to the emergency room sliding doors, she ran over and embraced him. "Your wife's going to pull through, William," Sherrie whispered to him. Then Sherrie pinched William in his back and said to him, "You're going to really owe your wife a true-to-heart apology, too!"

Turning to hug and thank Sherrie for coming to support him and his wife in their time of need, William replied to Sherrie, "Yes, I'm going to have a lot of making up to do. I've never disrespected my wife in that fashion. It's just been so much leading up to my outburst today that you're completely unaware of," William shared with Sherrie.

Even though William attempted to continue explaining to Sherrie about the issues that led to his behavior at his office earlier, it was to no avail. Sherrie had already deemed his earlier antics as inappropriate and unacceptable toward his wife. Sherrie hugged William and told him, "Let's just focus on your wife and what she needs at this time." William nodded and placed his head on Sherrie's shoulder.

If you truly knew William's heart, then you knew that he was suffering internally. William felt horrible for letting his emotions get the best of him. William was hurting because he had hurt his wife. William disrespected his wife, humiliated her and caused her to lose consciousness. Now he was standing in the hospital emergency room awaiting words from a doctor about his wife's condition.

The guilt of his actions were eating deep within William. He started saying to Sherrie, "This is all my fault. How could I have been so selfish?"

Sherrie was trying to calm William down. So she convinced him to take a walk with her down the hall so she could talk to him.

By this time Tabitha had made it to the hospital. Mike had been waiting out front for her. As soon as she found somewhere to park, her and Mike headed inside to go and check on their friends.

The moment that Tabitha got within speaking distance to her husband Mike, she was asking him what happened. Mike placed his arm around his wife and calmly replied, "You know as much as I do right now, baby."

Tabitha put her head on Mike's shoulder and they continued walking down the hall until they ran into Sherrie consoling William in the hallway.

Not sure who Sherrie was, Tabitha looked at Mike, then William and back to Sherrie.

Mike spoke up and said to his wife, "Sherrie is William's assistant. She was in William's office with him and Keisha before she lost consciousness."

Sherrie extended her hand to greet Tabitha, instead she received a half-smile from Tabitha.

Although it was apparent that Tabitha didn't feel Sherrie's presence was necessary at the hospital, Sherrie followed the crowd back into the waiting room as Tabitha had suggested they should go sit and await a report from the doctor.

No sooner than they stepped back into the waiting room, the doctor was calling William's name. William scurried over to the doctor with a mouth full of questions.

"Sir, please calm down," the doctor said to William. Then the doctor revealed to William that his wife had a heart attack.

William grabbed the doctor by his jacket and said, "No, no, that's not possible!"

The doctor tried yet failed to pull himself away from William's grasp. The doctor yelled for security!

The ruckus between the doctor and William prompted Mike, Tabitha and Sherrie to come over and intervene. Mike immediately separated William away from the doctor before security arrived.

Tabitha quickly apologized to the doctor on behalf of William. "He's a bit overwhelmed, again our sincerest of apologies to you, sir."

The doctor replied that he understood while straightening his jacket. Security arrived and the doctor waved them off, saying, "All's clear." Both security guards left without saying a word.

Extending her hand to the doctor and introducing herself as Keisha's sister, Tabitha learned that his name was Dr. Harper. Tabitha asked Dr. Harper, "Is Keisha stable, critical, conscious, unconscious or what?"

Dr. Harper shared with Tabitha that Keisha had a heart attack, yet she was conscious. Tabitha instantly put both hands to her mouth in shock!

"Was she under any stress that you know of?" the doctor asked Tabitha.

"Normal everyday stuff," Tabitha replied.

"Well, she's going to need some time to recover. So I suggest letting her get some rest before allowing any visitors," Dr. Harper said.

Tabitha nodded that she understood and thanked Dr. Harper before joining the others to apprise them of what she had just learned.

Joining the others, Tabitha explained to the group the exact information that she had just been given from Dr. Harper. Mike stepped up and hugged his wife because he could hear the emotion in her voice. Mike held Tabitha close to him and he rubbed his hand delicately in circles throughout the middle of her back. Her body sunk into his arms.

It didn't take much time at all before Tabitha approached William, asking him, "Why did you attack the doctor like that?"

William apologized to everyone for the way that he responded. Then he said to the group, "He told me that my wife had a heart attack and I just lost it!"

Tabitha reached out to hug William, then she said to him, "Had you remained poised and continued listening, you would've heard the latter of her condition."

After taking a glance at Sherrie, Tabitha returned her focus to William and said, "Keisha needs you to be strong for her right now." Tabitha touched his chest and said, "So control your emotions and be that take-charge man that Keisha fell in love with."

William hugged Tabitha, thanked her and assured her that he'd pull himself together.

Turning away from William, Tabitha sat down next to her husband. Mike put his arm around Tabitha and kissed her softly on her forehead.

"Everything's going to work itself out for the better," Mike said to William.

"And you have all of the support that you need right here with you," Sherrie said, while walking over to hug William.

That instantly triggered a reaction from Tabitha! Standing up, she asked, "Sherrie, excuse me, but who are you again? And why are you all up in the emergency room hugging on my best friend's husband?"

Sherrie quickly fired back, "I'm William's assistant. The one that came running into William's office to perform CPR on your best friend when she passed out. I'm here for support and praying that she makes it through," Sherrie responded to Tabitha.

Hearing all of that made Tabitha sit down momentarily. She crossed her legs and her foot was rocking at a rapid pace. Tabitha looked at her husband Mike and sarcastically shook her head repeatedly, saying, "If I wasn't saved…."

Mike hugged his wife and pulled her close to him, saying, "You're making more to this than it is, baby. There's absolutely nothing going on between William and Sherrie," Mike assured his wife.

Tabitha glanced over at William and Sherrie and said, "It better not be!"

"How are you holding up over here, William?" Sherrie asked.

"Trying to get my nerves and emotions both to settle," replied William. "I don't know what I was thinking. I really allowed my emotions to get the best of me," William said to Sherrie. "I need to apologize to my wife, physically hug her and know that everything is going to be alright," said William.

Sherrie patted William's thigh and stood up to walk towards the ladies' restroom.

Not a word came from Tabitha's lips, yet the way her eyes followed Sherrie to the bathroom were something treacherous. It was no secret that Tabitha had an issue with Sherrie's presence in the emergency room. Tabitha tapped Mike on his leg so that he'd lift his arm from around her, then she excused herself to walk over and talk to William.

Once Tabitha made her way over to where William was sitting, she sarcastically asked him, "Please tell me why your assistant has to be here with us while your wife's back there fighting for her life? I couldn't just sit over there pretending, I need to know, William, are you messing around with your assistant?"

It frustrated Tabitha more because William just sat there and didn't respond. So she began ranting, "I really thought you were different, William! As many times as I defended you to your wife," Tabitha said. "'No, he's different, Keisha, you have a special kind of man and he really loves you,'" Tabitha said mockingly.

"The main person that was pushing for you and Keisha to sit down and talk was me," said Tabitha. "I believed in you! That's why I was calling you earlier. Well. now I see why you didn't answer your phone, you were too busy with Ms. Thing," Tabitha said. "I was so wrong about you. And Keisha deserves better," Tabitha said.

"First of all, I didn't answer your calls because I didn't recognize the number that was calling me," William replied to Tabitha. "Secondly, I tried talking to my wife in our driveway and she still was treating me like she hated me. Third, I'm not messing around with my assistant. Lastly, I've never broken our vows. And I don't know one man that would still be standing faithfully by his wife with all that I've endured over this past year," William said.

Noticing that the exchange between Tabitha and William was getting a little heated, Mike walked over and asked his wife to step out into the hallway with him. Tabitha reluctantly obliged.

While Mike and Tabitha were walking out towards the hallway, Sherrie was returning from the restroom. The two ladies exchanged unpleasant looks in one another's direction, yet no words were spoken.

Once they were in the hallway, Mike decided to take his wife outside to get some fresh air. Also Mike knew he needed to talk to Tabitha so he could ease the tension in the emergency room.

"Before you even get started, Mike, l don't agree with her being here. And nothing you're about to say to me is going to change how I feel about the situation," Tabitha said. "I'm a woman, Mike, and I trust my intuition," Tabitha stood firmly telling her husband.

After hearing his wife rant about her women's intuition not stirring her wrong, Mike said to Tabitha, "This is the one time that your vibe is all wrong, baby. William isn't the least bit interested in Sherrie," Mike said. "That's the same man that drank himself to a crying frenzy on our couch last night over his wife and their issues," Mike told his wife.

"Now do you really believe that any man that hasn't received any action whatsoever from his wife in over a year that was cheating with another woman would be on his best friend's couch crying?" Mike asked Tabitha.

Before Tabitha could respond, Mike replied, "I don't think so. A guy wouldn't be crying over what he wasn't getting at home if he was actually getting it from somewhere outside of home," Mike told his wife.

Tabitha shook her head and told Mike, "You have a point."

Turning his head to the side, Mike looked at Tabitha side-eyed. "Okay, Mike, maybe I overreacted a little bit," Tabitha responded.

"A little bit?" Mike sarcastically asked Tabitha.

"Keisha is my best friend, how did you expect me to act?" asked Tabitha.

Mike kissed his wife on the lips, squeezed her hand gently, and Tabitha said, "Okay, I'll apologize to William, yet not his assistant."

Mike replied, "That's a start, baby."

Chapter Fifteen
Tables Turned

Meanwhile back inside of the hospital, Sherrie was asking William why Mike's wife was having an issue with her. William just shrugged it off, replying that he didn't know what Tabitha's issue was. "Aside from the fact that her and Keisha are best friends," William told Sherrie.

Nodding her head and now equipped with the knowledge of what the problem was, Sherrie said out loud, "Now I understand all of the animosity coming from Tabitha."

Somewhat puzzled by Sherrie's words, the confusion was noticeable on William's face. "Being that Tabitha is Keisha's best friend, she felt some type of way with me being here supporting her friend's husband and she doesn't even know who I am," Sherrie said. "I'm a woman, William, I better understand the reasoning for Tabitha's actions," Sherrie said.

"Wait a minute. You're my assistant, Sherrie. And the incident happened in my office where you were assisting at the time that it occurred. So why wouldn't you be here to support me and my wife?" asked William.

"Understand this, though, William, you and Mike know me, his wife doesn't know me from a slice of bread. Being a woman myself, I clearly understand her concerns. And I'm sure she'd really be unhappy if she knew that I rode to the hospital with her husband," Sherrie said to William.

Speaking of which, William nodded his head to Sherrie in the direction of Tabitha and Mike walking back into the emergency room. "There's some things that we need to address and clear up immediately," William said.

Accompanied by her husband Mike, Tabitha walked right up to William and apologized to him for her prior behavior in the emergency room. Tabitha hugged William and said, "I know you're going through more than enough right now. You don't need me adding to any of that. Our love and support is what you need. And we're here for you and Keisha in your time of need," Tabitha said.

Thank you, Tabitha and Mike, for understanding and caring enough to be here for me and my wife," William replied. "I really appreciate your continued friendship and support on both of our behalf. I know that everyone here is pulling for my wife to fully recover," William responded.

"However, after a brief dialogue with my assistant Sherrie while the two of you had stepped outside, I also feel there's a bit of a misunderstanding that we need to clear up in regards to that as well," continued William.

Tabitha took a step back and looked at her husband Mike, then she returned her attention and focus to William.

"Hold on, William," Sherrie politely interrupted. "I'd like to speak to Tabitha myself," Sherrie spoke up and said to William. Stepping over closer to Tabitha, Sherrie began explaining that she understood that Keisha and Tabitha were best friends. Sherrie also let Tabitha know how she as a woman understood the hostility.

However, Sherrie made it transparent to Tabitha that there was nothing openly or privately going on between her and her boss William. Sherrie further accounted for her being present at the emergency room was largely due to the fact that she was performing CPR on Keisha.

Reaching out to stop Sherrie from saying any more, Tabitha embraced, hugged and thanked Sherrie for stepping in to help her best friend Keisha. "You have just as much right to be here for support as anyone else standing here," Tabitha said to Sherrie.

One of the nurses came over to address the group. "The doctor will allow two of you at a time to come back and visit with the patient," the nurse said. "Which two will it be?" asked the nurse.

It was quickly decided that William and Tabitha would be the first two visitors to see Keisha. The nurse told William and Tabitha, "Please follow me."

The walk towards the room where Keisha was resting had William's stomach in knots. He suddenly became nervous and somewhat uneasy. Tabitha seemed calm and anxious to witness that her friend was alright. She looked at William and could immediately sense his sudden anxiety.

Tabitha grabbed William's hand and said, "Everything's going to be okay. I'm right here with you for support."

In an attempt to show good faith, William flashed a confident smile and nodded his head in the direction of Tabitha. She squeezed his hand lightly, then they both walked into the room where Keisha was hooked to machines.

Without question, Tabitha instantly walked over to the bed where Keisha was lying. Tabitha gently picked up Keisha's hand and said, "We're right here by your side, bestie."

William was standing by the door fighting back the emotions that were roaring up inside of him.

More than anything, it was the guilt and shame that was overwhelming William at the moment. He felt as though his wife wouldn't be laying before him in this bed in this predicament if it weren't for him succumbing to his own selfish will.

The thoughts that were rummaging through William's mind weren't helping his current situation any at all. He kept wondering what he would do if his wife passed away. Who would help him raise their kids? Would he ever be happy again? Would he ever be able to forgive himself for being the reason that she died? How would he explain this to their children?

Even though William didn't actually murder their mom, in his mind he was convinced that he would've been guilty for killing her by breaking her heart. And he stood there lost in a trance because he couldn't live with that on his conscience.

Besides the obvious, William honestly loved his wife! Although he allowed his anger to cause him to say some dreadful things, never in his existence did William want to imagine living a day on this earth without his wife by his side.

So William finally walked over to the bed where Keisha was laying and he took ahold of her other hand. William placed his opposite hand on top of Keisha's hand and began rubbing it passionately. Tabitha smiled at William and nodded her approval.

Not sure where to begin, William asked Tabitha, "Do you think Keisha can hear me right now?"

Before Tabitha had a chance to respond to William's question, Keisha delicately squeezed her husband's hand as an indication that she could hear him.

Flushed with a renewed vigor, William began apologizing to Keisha for the way that he talked to her, treated her and promised her that he'd never act so selfishly and foolishly ever again. William got down on one knee and begged his wife for forgiveness. Keisha squeezed William's hand twice. And when William stood up he was delighted to see that his wife's eyes were now open and she was smiling.

"That was very sweet, loving, touching and thoughtful of you, William," Keisha responded. "You really hurt me with your words and how you treated me in your office," Keisha told William.

"However, after the way I've behaved and neglected your needs as your wife since I gave birth to our son, how can I blame you?" Keisha asked William. "I don't know any man that would still be standing faithfully by his wife's side after how I've treated you over this past year."

William bent down and kissed his wife on the forehead. That brought a huge smile to Keisha's face.

"Now this is truly a sight to see," Tabitha said. She pulled out her cell phone and took a picture of William holding Keisha's hand and kissing her on her lips. "That's how a husband stands by his wife's side and remains true to the oath that he took before God," Tabitha continued rambling on. "I love it, I love it, I absolutely love it," Tabitha said very proudly!

"Whew," Tabitha shouted out as she started fanning herself. "The two of you have gotten me all emotional up in this hospital."

William broke his embrace with his wife to grab some Kleenex for Tabitha.

"Thank you, William," Tabitha sighed.

"You're welcome," William replied. Then he locked hands with Keisha and began running his fingers through her hair.

That made Keisha relax as she felt the tender touch of her husband playfully running his fingers through her hair and gingerly massaging her scalp. Keisha had forgotten how intriguing she found William's touch. His strong masculine hands were always soothing when he touched her.

Without realizing what he was doing, William had begun caressing his wife's neck, running his fingers ever so slowly around her earlobes and stroking the sides of her face delicately with the back of his hand.

Little did William know, he was arousing his wife with every touch of his fingers on her upper body. Keisha's breathing grew heavier with every fine touch. Her body began squirming as the sensations were racking through her body.

The sudden movements Keisha was making in the bed alarmed William. He mistook the pleasure that Keisha was receiving from his soft touches for her being uncomfortable. Panicking, William asked Keisha, "Are you uncomfortable? Do you want me to summon the nurse?"

Letting out a soft giggle, Keisha whispered to William, "You were touching my spot and I got a little excited under these sheets."

Tabitha and Keisha laughed in unison.

"Don't make me climb under these sheets with you in this hospital," William told Keisha.

"Excuse me, but that's my cue to give the two of you some alone time in this room," Tabitha said. Standing up and walking out, she turned and said, "Don't get arrested in this hospital."

Keisha and William laughed as Tabitha left them alone.

Focusing his attention back to his wife, William ran his index finger over Keisha's lips, over the bridge of her nose and around the contours of her face. Keisha started writhing, moaning and telling William how much she missed his touch. William responded telling his wife how much he missed touching her, pleasing her and seeing her satisfied.

The two of them locked eyes for the first time in more than a year. Keisha had tears in her eyes. William noticed it, wiped her tears away and asked her, "Baby, what's wrong?"

Keisha shook her head from side to side, causing a few more tears to escape from her beautiful mysterious eyes, then she responded, "I just realized how much I love you and took you for granted, William."

Bending down to hug Keisha, William looked her square in her eyes and said, "I missed hearing you say that, baby." Then he kissed his wife softly on her full lips.

Keisha responded with some passion of her own. William stepped back for a second admiring his wife. Keisha bit her lip and winked at her husband. William stepped closer to the bed and kissed his wife passionately yet seductively.

Clearing her throat to alarm the couple that she entered the room, the nurse said, "I see someone's feeling a lot better."

Breaking their love embrace, Keisha responded, "This fine husband of mine seems to be all that I really needed!"

The nurse looked at William, then back to Keisha and jokingly said, "I don't blame you, not one bit."

Both women laughed, then William cleared his throat, indicating that he was still present in the room. "Excuse me for my unprofessionalism, Mr. Johnson, I'm here to check your wife's vitals," the nurse responded.

Then the nurse and Keisha shared a quick wink as she began checking Keisha's vitals.

Chapter Sixteen
Playing the Game

Passing time in the waiting room, Tabitha and Sherrie were talking and laughing. Tabitha was content with knowing that her friend Keisha was conscious and showing signs of recovering rather quickly. Tabitha looked at Sherrie and sincerely thanked her for stepping up and assisting with Keisha. Sherrie assured Tabitha that it was no trouble.

While the two ladies continued small talking and sharing stories, Mike had slipped out into the hallway and was talking on the phone to the girl Tiffany that he'd met at the restaurant earlier in the day.

Having little to no respect for his wife, Mike was trying to convince Tiffany to meet him at the hospital so the two of them could slip away unnoticed.

Never having revealed that he was married, Tiffany had no idea that Mike was married. Nor had she asked him. Mike's motto with the women that he dealt with outside of his wife was if they didn't ask, he didn't mention that he was married.

After some very persuasive flirting on the phone, Mike had successfully talked Tiffany into coming to meet him at the hospital. Tiffany was turned on at the thought of possibly getting caught in the act in such a busy public place. It was the hint of danger along with the wild streak deep within her that Tiffany found intriguing.

With the challenging and naughty thoughts of her quest to conquer Mike, Tiffany threw on a short, tight-fitting mini dress with no panties underneath, sprayed some intoxicating sweet-smelling perfume on and headed to meet Mike at the destination that he requested.

Even though Mike viewed Tiffany as just another potentially good piece of pleasure at his leisure, Tiffany had her own secret agenda. Tiffany had a plan of pleasuring Mike beyond what he was used to in hopes of gaining continual access to his openly noticeable spending habits.

In Tiffany's mind she would meet with Mike whenever he summoned her to and have no limits to satisfy him. Tiffany was a spontaneous type of woman and Mike was a flashy show-off type of guy. It was a match made that would go well, or so Tiffany thought.

During the time that Mike was waiting for Tiffany to text his cell phone and let him know that she had arrived, Mike had returned to the waiting room to socially mingle with his wife and Sherrie. Mike cracked a couple of jokes and had both of the ladies laughing.

Without a doubt, Mike wasn't the nicest-looking guy, yet his personality and his sense of humor would often win over a crowd of women. Not to mention his status. Mike had money and was known to flaunt his assets to get what he wanted from women. He was a big tipper and a big spender.

Meaning Mike had no problem with spending money on his female counterparts. Mike was boastful and liked to make it apparent to the women that he dealt with that money wasn't a problem for him.

Some would say that it attracted the wrong females to him for all of the wrong reasons. Yet that was always Mike's catch and aim in the selection of women that he often engaged and interacted with all while cheating on his wife. Mike thrived on the women that he could manipulate with his financial approach.

At home, Mike and Tabitha were seldom intimate and not really in love anymore. It had grown to be a marriage where Tabitha would have relations with Mike without even relating to him. When Mike wanted to be intimate, against her better judgment, Tabitha would willingly comply just to satisfy his urges. And it did nothing to stop him from cheating on her.

Although Tabitha had a hidden suspicion that Mike was cheating on her with other women, she ignored her womanly instincts because he took care of home and she feared starting over on her own. Mike was a great provider, yet a horrible husband.

Therefore, Tabitha often put her emotions aside and just accepted life as it came with Mike. She chose stability over all else. So Tabitha would never concern herself with anything that Mike was entertaining outside of their household.

If in fact Mike was partaking in affairs with other women, Tabitha didn't want to know about it. Because she knew how she'd respond if he ever got messy and allowed his clumsiness to spill over before her eyes.

Make no mistake about it, Tabitha knew that Mike loved her. And she also loved her husband. However, the fact that Tabitha was raised amongst her brothers and had seen the lying, cheating and manipulating ways of men from many different angles somewhat prepared her for her future relationships with men.

Therefore, Tabitha wasn't oblivious to the underlying realities of a cheating man. Her brothers taught her that just because a man loves you doesn't mean that he won't cheat on you. A man can completely take care of home and feel that he's entitled to cheat at his leisure. So she knew to selectively choose what she would accept and deal with.

Looking at Mike in the waiting room, Tabitha could sense that something was different about his demeanor. She couldn't quite put a finger on it right offhand, yet she knew that something was different within him.

Even though Mike was engaging in conversation with his wife and Sherrie, he was constantly checking his phone like he was expecting a call from someone specifically. Tabitha noticed Mike's jittery mannerism with his phone, yet she didn't say anything.

The conversation went from joking and laughing to serious when William came walking out towards Mike, Tabitha and Sherrie with a perturbed look on his face.

Immediately Tabitha and Sherrie rushed up to William, asking him, "Is everything alright with Keisha?"

William nodded his head yes, that everything was alright with Keisha.

Then Tabitha asked William, "Well, is everything alright with you?"

Again William nodded his head yes, that everything was alright with him as well.

"So what's the reason for the worried expression on your face, William?" asked Tabitha.

Before William could respond, Mike interrupted, saying, "How about you two ladies go back and visit with Keisha and I'll take William on a walk and talk with him. This all can be a bit overwhelming, maybe he just needs a break and some fresh air. Would either of you ladies like anything to eat or drink?" asked Mike.

"No, we're fine," both ladies responded.

"Suit yourself," Mike replied.

"I don't know about the ladies, but I can certainly use a drink right now," William said.

Mike patted his friend on the back and replied, "I might have something in my truck for you."

At that moment, William and Mike began walking out of the emergency room towards where Mike had parked his truck. The fellas didn't quite make it outside before Mike's text message notification went off.

Pulling out his phone to check his message, Mike realized that Tiffany had texted him notifying him that she had arrived at the hospital. Mike whispered to William what he was about to do. William shook his head in disbelief, then asked Mike for the keys to his truck so he could get to the bottle of liquor that was in his truck. Mike tossed William his keys and proceeded to meet up with Tiffany.

Standing there watching Mike walk away to go and cheat with Tiffany while his wife Tabitha was inside of the hospital had William contemplating, could he ever do that to his wife Keisha> Quickly deciding that wasn't in his character to do, William unlocked Mike's truck and sat inside once he retrieved the bottle of liquor.

Walking towards Tiffany's car, Mike inserted a piece of chewing gum into his mouth to make certain that his breath was fresh before approaching Tiffany's vehicle.

Once Mike made it to Tiffany's car door, he opened her car door as a gentleman is supposed to. His mouth fell open when he saw the revealing mini dress that Tiffany had on as she stepped out of her car.

Holding Tiffany's hand, Mike spun her around to get an all-around visual of how dynamic her figure was accentuated in this short lovely ensemble. The miniskirt hugged Tiffany's hips expertly. Her posterior was protruding profoundly through her skirt. Her legs were sleek and oiled up. Tiffany's succulent bosom was literally popping out of her dress.

Shaking his head in sheer disbelief, Mike took Tiffany into his arms and hugged her tightly. He kissed her softly on the lips, then more passionately as the two were locked in a hot and steamy lip lock.

Grabbing Tiffany by her hand, Mike led her into the hospital. He pointed and whispered in her ear where the two of them were going to go one after the other to finish what they had just started.

With no hesitation at all, Tiffany walked directly over to the family restroom as instructed by Mike. She locked the door and waited to hear Mike knock lightly three times so she'd know to let him in.

Taking his time to observe the area and make certain that no one was watching Tiffany go into the family restroom, Mike then hurriedly walked over and lightly knocked on the door three times. Tiffany unlocked the door, then stepped back, giving Mike access into the restroom, where she was anxiously waiting for him.

Meanwhile, after having taken more than a few sips out of the bottle of liquor in Mike's truck, William decided to head back into the hospital and check on his wife Keisha. So William locked the now open bottle in Mike's trunk.

First William inserted a couple of breath mints into his mouth to cover up the scent of liquor on his breath. Then he headed back inside the hospital towards the emergency room.

Chapter Seventeen
Signs and Symbols

When William reached the emergency room waiting area, Sherrie was sitting alone in a corner with her head down crying. William walked over to Sherrie, started rubbing her back and asked her why she was crying. Sherrie looked up at William with her eyes full of tears and just pointed towards the general area where Keisha was.

After a few uneducated guesses, William figured out that Sherrie was trying to tell him that the problem was with his wife Keisha.

With nothing else needing to be said, William rushed over to the emergency room doors, pressed the button and was granted access through. William's mind began racing frantically as he was taking the necessary steps to reach the room where his wife was supposedly resting.

Before William reached the doorway to the room where his wife was lying in bed, Tabitha stepped out into the hallway and hugged him tightly to prevent him from entering the room. William could feel Tabitha sobbing against his chest. He immediately sought to comfort her.

However, the sudden change in behavior from Sherrie and Tabitha from when William had just left them in the visiting room in an upbeat mood alarmed William and heightened his senses. Tabitha whispered in William's ear and his body went stiff.

Knowing that William really loved his wife, was a highly emotional man and would be devastated by the thought of losing her, Tabitha made a conscious decision to walk William back out to the waiting room and talk to him privately.

It was a very slow walk for William and Tabitha through the double doors and outside into the hallway. Tabitha was prolonging the walk so she could think of how she'd approach William with the conversation that the two of them needed to have before he went into the room to see his wife.

While passing through the emergency room waiting area, Tabitha stopped to see how Sherrie was holding up. Sherrie stood up, gave Tabitha a hug and asked her, "How are you holding up?" Tabitha assured Sherrie that she was alright. Then Tabitha motioned with her head towards William, indicating that she wasn't so sure about him, though.

Whispering to Tabitha, Sherrie asked, "Does William know?"

Tabitha shook her head no in Sherrie's direction. "We're about to walk and talk now," Tabitha said.

"Do you want me to come along?" Sherrie asked.

"Being that you're already aware of the situation that I need to talk to him about and you have an established relationship with William, yes, I'd appreciate you joining us on our stroll and talk," Tabitha told Sherrie.

Picking up her pocketbook, Sherrie got up and started walking with Tabitha and William towards the hallway. Sherrie locked eyes with William and sorrow overtook her instantly.

On one side Tabitha had her arm locked in William's. And Sherrie had her arm locked in William's on the other side. Both Tabitha and Sherrie had their heads resting on either side of William's shoulders.

Dragging his feet and filled with suspense, yet not wanting to ask the obvious question, William sort of fell in stride with Tabitha and Sherrie for the time being.

The three of them together had been walking back and forth up and down the hallway in silence with no words being spoken between them for quite some time until Tabitha stated that she needed to use the restroom.

Pointing ahead of the direction that they were walking, Sherrie said, "There's a family restroom just ahead of us."

Tabitha unhooked her arm from William's and began walking at a feverish pace to the restroom.

As Tabitha approached the restroom door and turned the knob, her mouth fell open when she saw her husband Mike coming out of the restroom holding Tiffany's hand.

It seemed like time froze for approximately five seconds or so. William had no clue that Mike was taking Tiffany inside of the hospital to fornicate with her. William thought the two of them were leaving in Tiffany's car.

Standing there shaking her head in disbelief, Sherrie unhooked her arm from William's and stood behind him to shield herself from harm's way.

Having not caught on yet, Tiffany was the first to speak. Hands on her hips, Tiffany asked, "Mike, can you tell me what's going on?"

Tabitha spoke up and asked, "Yes, Mike, please tell us what's going on here?"

Mike looked at William, and Tabitha asked Mike, "Why are you looking at William?"

Noticing William from earlier, Tiffany said, "Hey, William."

Tabitha turned to William with a menacing expression on her face and asked, "Oh, so you know about this little arrangement too, William?"

Without responding, William just walked away. This was none of William's business and he wasn't about to get dragged into it. He felt a sense of regret for his friend Mike. Yet William had always told Mike that he was careless and would eventually get caught.

Not to mention that William never supported Mike cheating on his wife in the first place. Mike often used excuses, telling William the things that Tabitha wasn't doing at home were the reasons he sought after random women outside of his marriage.

Many times Mike would tell William that he was just different than most guys. Mike even joked sometimes, calling William an alien and saying that he wasn't from this planet.

Further stating that no man would repeatedly be denied the simple pleasures from his wife and not go obtaining it from elsewhere. Saying strange things like "If my wife lets me leave the house unsatisfied, I've got a woman that'll take care of the very things that she's neglecting to take care of at home," Mike would often boast about to William.

"When my wife gets in one of her moods and decides that she doesn't want to cook for me, I've got several women that I can call that'll get out of their bed and make me a homecooked meal at three o'clock in the morning," Mike would brag often to William.

"When me and my wife are at odds and she decides she wants to give me the silent treatment, I don't worry not one strand of hair on my head. I just text or call one of my little lady friends, talk and flirt with them every day until my wife gets over whatever it is that upset her," Mike would say to William.

"When my wife has those times when she's feeling some type of way and doesn't want to satisfy my physical appetite, she's sending me outside of the house with my testosterone elevated," Mike would always say to William.

"The fact that I take care of home and none of my wife's needs are being neglected, none of my needs will ever be neglected either," Mike would say. "Whether my wife takes care of my needs or I have to seek to fulfill my needs outside of our home, I won't sit around waiting for something from her that I can go get anytime that I want it outside of our home," Mike would often say.

With that thought, William could remember times that Mike used to cheat with a woman that lived around the corner from his home with his wife. Mike even cheated with a woman that lived across the street from him in the same bed that he and his wife slept in while his wife was at work!

In fact, there were several women working in William and Mike's office that Mike had slept with as well. Random pickups from bars, nightclubs, restaurants, even a couple of women from grocery stores. Mike was truly a hound.

There were many different women that Mike had random affairs with out of Tabitha's sight. And up until this moment, he had never been caught up with another woman.

Still somehow maintaining her poise, Tabitha asked the lady standing there with her husband, "What's your name, sweetheart?"

Tiffany told Tabitha her name with no hesitation.

Then Tabitha asked, "Tiffany, did my husband tell you that he was married?"

"Married!" Tiffany yelled. "No, he didn't tell me that he was married,"

Tiffany responded, then pushed Mike violently into the restroom door.

After apologizing to Tabitha, Tiffany, embarrassed by the whole ordeal, walked away crying. Tabitha didn't blink not once while Tiffany walked away. All of her attention and focus was on the one that owed her the respect, her husband.

"Do you care to explain to me why we're here in the hospital praying for Keisha, who's back there fighting for her life, and you're out here jumping up and down in some tight-dress-wearing female that you picked up from God knows where?" Tabitha asked Mike.

Arrogantly Mike looked at Tabitha and said, "We're not about to discuss this in public. We'll talk about this later at home," Mike said, pounding his fist against the restroom door.

"No, no, we won't talk about this later at home," Tabitha replied while taking steps backwards away from Mike. "Because your home is no longer my home."

Taking off her ring and throwing it at Mike, Tabitha shouted, "I don't want this lopsided marriage anymore, Michael! I'm moving out immediately! And I'm filing for divorce!" Tabitha yelled, then walked off.

Sherrie looked at Mike with a look of sheer disgust, then quickly scurried behind Tabitha to offer her comfort and support in her time of need.

Locked in an intense stare-off, Mike and William just stood there looking at one another. About ten seconds after, William turned and walked off, leaving Mike standing in his own pity. Mike pounded his fist against the wall several times before bending down to pick up his wife's wedding ring.

Chapter Eighteen
The Collapse

Never did Mike imagine living life without his wife Tabitha. All of the time that Mike was selfishly partaking in his extramarital affairs, he took for granted the strain it would put on his marriage.

Having never taken his wife's feelings into account, Mike was now stuck in the hallway contemplating, should he go after his wife or give her time to process everything as a whole? Not really sure what to do at the time, Mike just slid down the wall and sat there with his head in his hands.

Knowing that he had messed up drastically, Mike wondered, would Tabitha leave him for good or was she just angry with him for the moment?

For once, Mike found himself overwhelmed and engulfed in a cloud of uncertainty. A man that was always sure of himself was now left to feel empty, lonely, shameful and incomplete.

Many people were walking by, yet Mike felt like he was the only person in the hallway at the moment. It was like everything just slowed down and was moving in slow motion.

Bowing his head on the cold hospital floor that he was now kneeling on, Mike began repenting, praying to God and asking Him to please put it on Tabitha's heart to forgive him and take him back.

Hearing his text notification going off several times brought Mike out of the trance that he was locked in. He stood himself up and went back into the family restroom to get himself together.

After blowing his nose a few times, Mike began washing his face and hands in the sink. He took a long look at himself in the mirror and felt a sudden sweep of shame overtake him.

Not one to pity himself much or beat himself up over things that he couldn't control, Mike took a deep breath, dried his hands and pulled out his cell phone.

The notifications that were simultaneously alerting Mike's phone were all from his wife Tabitha. She told him that she couldn't believe that he had the audacity to cheat on her in the hospital in front of their friends while one of their friends was fighting for her life in the emergency room.

Each text message got heavier, more personal and deeply emotional. Tabitha was all over the place with her messages.

One minute Tabitha was texting Mike, asking him how could he have acted so selfishly, disrespected her in front of their friends, telling him how much she hated him, that she'd never ever trust him again and she never wanted to ever see him again.

Next minute Tabitha was texting Mike, telling him after things got situated here in the hospital with Keisha, that the two of them needed to sit down and talk. Tabitha was telling Mike that he owed her a sincere apology and he needed to promise that he'd never hurt her like that again.

Noticing that Tabitha was willing to forgive him, Mike started texting Tabitha, apologizing to her and promising her that he'd never ever do anything selfish or stupid to hurt her again. Mike also told Tabitha that he agreed that the two of them needed to talk.

While texting back and forth with Tabitha, Mike received a text message from Tiffany. Feeling content with where things were heading with his wife Tabitha, Mike decided to respond to Tiffany's text message.

Tiffany texted Mike, apologizing for causing problems with his wife. She told him if he needed her for anything, he knew how to reach her. She also told him that he could've been honest with her about being married and she would've respected boundaries. Saying that it wouldn't have affected their dealings with one another.

Beforehand Mike was under the impression that he had lost his wife and his new potential love interest. The thought of that alone had him down in the dumps. Mike really loved his wife. And even though he cheated on her many times, he didn't want to lose her. Or was it that he didn't want to see her with anyone else?

However, now equipped with the knowledge that he wouldn't lose his wife, nor the beautiful woman that he just had an affair with, Mike would tell his wife what she wanted to hear and be wiser how he interacted with Tiffany.

Being that Tiffany was alright with dealing with Mike, even though he was married, Mike wouldn't have to lie, manipulate or be secretive with Tiffany. For she made it known that she had no reservations about discreetly having an open affair with him. And never causing any strife between him and his wife.

Adjusting his blazer and replacing the previous scowl on his face with a huge smile, Mike's confidence and vigor was renewed just that quickly.

That moment clarified one thing for certain, Mike would never stop cheating on his wife! Tabitha's confusion with what she felt for Mike combined with what she was being dealt from Mike would harbor her ability to make and stand firm on rash decisions pertaining to her marriage with Mike.

Therefore, Mike would be able to engage in extramarital affairs whenever he so desired with women like Tiffany at his leisure without having to worry about potentially losing his wife. Because his wife feared losing the one person that she loved and she knew loved her no matter what he did outside of their home because she feared being alone.

Although Tabitha would get upset, tell Mike that it was over and she didn't want to be married to him anymore, each time she forgave him and walked back into that same marriage without seeking adequate counseling with a man that didn't respect his wife nor the vows that he took, she was allowing him to cheat.

There's so many women in this world that live, think and feel the same way as Tiffany does. Some guys are going to cheat regardless of how good their woman is to them.

No matter how good looking his woman is, no matter how supportive she is to her man, no matter how often she satisfies him and makes sure he never wants for anything, some guys are still going to cheat.

The woman in the relationship can make more money than her man, holding him down and going all out for him in every way, and some of these guys will still cheat with women that don't even have a car or still living at home with their parents.

Tiffany is one of many women in this world that'll knowingly sleep with married men or guys in relationships for her own selfish gain with no regard to the feelings of the wife or girlfriend.

Cheating is a selfish choice. And any woman that locks in and deals with a guy knowing that he's married or in a relationship is selfish in her choice to allow that man to cheat while cheating herself at the same time.

Men cheat because they're selfish! To inadequately make the choice time and time again to engage in acts that you know adversely affect the person that you claim you love is selfish. To not care about hurting someone you love is selfish.

A bad decision is a mistake. Mistakes can be forgiven. However, to continue to make the same bad decisions is a choice. And choices come with consequences.

The fact that some guys entertain the notion that it's not cheating unless you get caught validates that some guys feel it's appropriate to cheat as long as they're discreet about it. Cheating is wrong no matter your gender or sexual preference.

Chapter Nineteen
Broken

Somehow Tabitha and Sherrie found their way back to William just before he was about to walk through the double doors of the emergency room. Tabitha yelled out William's name. Hearing a familiar voice calling his name, William stopped, turned and looked to see who was yelling his name in the hospital.

Once he saw Tabitha and Sherrie, William started walking towards the ladies. Tabitha was no longer hesitant about what she needed to discuss with William.

"There's some things that we need to talk about, William, and they can't wait," Tabitha said.

William gestured to some chairs that were nearby.

After taking a seat, Tabitha looked at William and said, "There's some things that Keisha confided in me and asked me to never tell you unless she couldn't tell you herself, William."

Uncertainty boldly displaying on his face, William didn't say anything. He just channeled in his focus and listened to Tabitha while Sherrie sat close by for moral support.

Little did William know, he wasn't ready to hear none of the things that Tabitha was about to disclose to him.

Going back to when they first met, Tabitha asked William if he remembered asking Keisha how she felt about children. William nodded

127

his head, confirming that he did remember. Tabitha looked at Sherrie, then back to William before telling him the painful truth about Keisha's true reason for never wanting to have any children.

Holding up his hand, William asked Tabitha, "So why did Keisha lie to me early on, telling me that she wanted to have a big family when she knew that she didn't want to give birth to any children?"

"Because you were refreshing to her, William. And she didn't want to let you get away. The guys she dated before you were liars, losers and manipulators. Keisha saw something different in you. She always boasted that you were a special kind of man, much different than any other man that she'd ever met. She knew you were the one for her, William."

Hearing what Tabitha was telling him, yet still quite a bit rattled by some of the information that was just revealed to him, William had a few questions of his own.

"In all of the years that we've been together, Keisha never felt comfortable sitting down and sharing these things with me?" William asked Tabitha. "I'm not sure how I feel about all of this," William said. "I've kept no secrets from my wife. And after learning all of this new information, I'm not so sure that she hasn't kept more secrets from me," William continued.

"Now hold on, William," Tabitha said. "Keisha didn't withhold these painful hidden scars from her past from you to be dishonest or to hurt you. She was confused, in love and tried not to let her past have any effect on her future with you," Tabitha told William.

Both hands on his head, William asked Tabitha, "What else has Keisha been dreadfully withholding from me? I'm sure there's more," William said.

"The things that I'm telling you have embedded deep emotional scars within Keisha since her early childhood," Tabitha told William.

"The complications that she encountered during her last pregnancy triggered her PTSD," Tabitha revealed to William.

"Hence the reasons why Keisha indirectly lost her drive for intimacy and became emotionally withdrawn within your marriage," Tabitha continued.

"Wow!" exclaimed William. "This is a lot to process," William said. He stood up and started pacing nervously back and forth, saying, "I've been supportive of my wife through everything. And I have to admit it hasn't been easy as of late."

Gesturing with his hands and pointing at the ground, William said, "All of this new information is something altogether different, though. And I can't promise that I'll be as supportive as I have been. It's going to take a lot of prayer, faith and possibly even some counseling to weather this storm."

Nodding her head that she understood precisely William's response to what she had divulged to him so far, Tabitha couldn't help but to think to herself if William would explode once he heard the worst of it all about his wife Keisha.

However, it was no point of holding back, there was no better time than now to put all the cards on the table.

So after taking a series of deep breaths, Tabitha stopped William from pacing long enough to get his undivided attention to tell him that Keisha was raped and was afraid to tell him.

"Raped? When? And by who?" asked a noticeably agitated William. "Who raped my wife?" William asked again. "Tabitha, don't get quiet on me now, who raped my wife?" William asked much more aggressively. Gently grabbing Tabitha by her shoulders, William pleaded with her, "Please tell me who raped Keisha. I'll go and take care of that right now!" William said vehemently.

Tabitha couldn't even look William in his eyes. Her head down, tears running down her face, she just kept shaking her head no and pounding her clenched fist into her thigh.

Noticing how emotional that Tabitha had suddenly became moved William to put his arm around Tabitha in an attempt to comfort her. Sherrie was rubbing the palm of her right hand in circles along the middle of Tabitha's back to offer her support.

This episode went on for what seemed like minutes. William, with one of his arms around Tabitha rubbing her shoulder. His other hand was atop her hand, kneading it passively. Sherrie was whispering softly to Tabitha, "It's alright, you can tell him, it's time that he knows the whole truth."

Hearing Sherrie say those things made William even more anxious to hear the pertinent information that Tabitha was withholding. So William began trying to get Tabitha to relax so that he could get her to open up and reveal who was the person that raped his wife.

Sherrie and William made eye contact and were momentarily locked in an intense gaze. Neither said a word to the other. They casually spoke to one another with their eyes. Sherrie smiled big and bright at William. Then she rubbed his hand before breaking their eye contact to focus on Tabitha's wellbeing.

William was taken aback for a few about the minute exchange between himself and Sherrie. William had never viewed Sherrie in any other light other than as his assistant. However, William saw something different in Sherrie's eyes at that moment. Something that he hadn't ever noticed previous to now.

While Sherrie had channeled her focus to rubbing Tabitha's back and encouraging her to open all the way up to William, he himself had slipped off into his thoughts in attempts to make sense of what he was feeling at the moment.

Back and forth was William's thoughts. Could it be possible, how is it that he never noticed his attraction to Sherrie until now? *No, this couldn't be because I'm a married man*, William was thinking to himself.

Taking one last glance at Sherrie, William noticed that she was a very attractive woman with long naturally straight hair, almond-shaped eyes, full lips and an invitingly nice pretty white smile. All of those attributes complimented heavily by a curvaceous figure that most men drooled over. William couldn't help but to reflect on how earlier that day Sherrie had made a pass at him in his office.

Under different circumstances, William may have responded differently to Sherrie's acts of coming on to him. Yet he was a married man and he firmly believed in remaining faithful to his wife. William shook the subtle fantasies that he was entertaining in his mind about Sherrie and returned his undivided attention to Tabitha.

Touching Tabitha's hand, William asked her, "Are you feeling better?" Tabitha shook her head yes. William excused himself to go and retrieve some tissue for Tabitha.

The moment that William walked away, Tabitha turned and said to Sherrie, "As painful as it will be to tell him, I know that it's time that William knows the whole truth."

Sherrie continued rubbing Tabitha's back and replied, "Yes, it really is time that William knows the truth about everything."

In between sniffles, Tabitha responded, "William has been in the dark on some things for quite some time and I've harbored so much guilt by not coming forth and telling him out of respect for the privacy of friendship.

"The guilt swept over me heavily earlier today when Mike and William were asking me questions about Keisha," Tabitha revealed to Sherrie.

That raised an eyebrow on Sherrie.

"The two of them together?" asked Sherrie.

Tabitha nodded yes.

"And what exactly were they questioning you about?" asked Sherrie.

Raising her head to make eye contact with Sherrie, Tabitha slowly replied, "They asked me did I know why Keisha was being so distant and acting different towards William."

"And what did you tell them?" Sherrie asked.

"First of all, let me say this. It took everything within me not to emotionally unravel and just lay it all out on the table before both of them," Tabitha stated.

"However, I sucked it up and told them that Keisha would enlighten William when she was ready to openly discuss their situation," Tabitha continued speaking. "And I did empathize with William in regards to the neglect he was enduring within his marriage," Tabitha included.

Sherrie nodded her head and continued rubbing Tabitha on her back to bolster her strength to continue to speak.

"The whole time, Mike was standing right beside William playing the supportive friend role," Tabitha said with a look of disgust.

Sherrie turned her neck sideways and said, "The nerve of Mike!"

Just as those words had left Sherrie's mouth, William was returning with some tissue for Tabitha. Extending his arm to hand the tissue to Tabitha, William then turned his attention to Sherrie and nonchalantly asked, "What did Mike do now? Or do I even want to know?"

"Oh, there's some things that you need to know, William," Sherrie said while leaning forward in her chair towards William's way.

Looking at Sherrie, then back to Tabitha, "Can someone please level with me and stop with all of these riddles already?" William asked.

Patting the empty seat next to her, Tabitha gestured for William to sit down next to her. Taking a seat next to Tabitha, William pleaded with her to be honest with him about whatever it was that she knew and was withholding.

"William, I'm not sure how to tell you this," biting her lip, tears unexpectedly streaming down her face again, "yet I've known for a year now who the man was that raped Keisha and sent her into that mental state of depression, thus causing the separation in your marriage over the past year. Keisha sought counseling, therapy, fasting and praying. None of it was serving as any healing for her emotional, mental or social state."

William reached over and hugged Tabitha with one arm, his hand gently massaging her shoulder. His eyes full of tears now, William asked Tabitha to please continue.

"Keisha's suffering from rape trauma syndrome," Tabitha said to William. "Hence the changes in her physical, emotional, social, cognitive and interpersonal behavior, William," Tabitha continued to elaborate on the details of the condition that Keisha was diagnosed with. "Keisha has been struggling with a severe case of PTSD, high levels of anxiety and depression as a result of the unfortunate incident.

"So understand that it was nothing that you did to cause your wife to stop loving you or to lose her desire for you, William. That pure, sweet, innocent love that the two of you shared was taken from the two of you by a gutless, selfish coward!" Tabitha exclaimed.

By now William was crying with Tabitha as she continued to fight through her own anxiety and emotions of reliving the misery that had been haunting her friend Keisha. William stood up with both of his fists clenched tightly and asked Tabitha, "Who is the dead man that committed this horrendous act against my wife? I'll kill him," William whispered menacingly while pounding his fist against the hospital wall.

"That's what Keisha feared most, William. She thought she was protecting you by not telling you. So she opted to suffer in silence. The only person that she ever told what happened was me," Tabitha said.

Shaking his head no repeatedly, tears falling freely down either side of his face, William looked over to Sherrie and she had tears falling down her face as well.

Sherrie walked up to William and hugged him tightly, saying, "We're both here for you, William."

As comforting as it was to know that both Sherrie and Tabitha were there for him, it did little to nothing to numb the pain, rage and anger that was building within William by the moment.

Breaking their embrace, William stepped away from Sherrie and walked over to kneel in front of Tabitha. William lifted Tabitha's chin with two fingers so that the two of them would be making direct eye contact. Tabitha's body was shaking uncontrollably, tears covering her face. William took the tissue from Tabitha's hand and began drying the wet tears that had saturated her face.

Tabitha looked deep into William's eyes. Then she reached out and placed both of her hands on top of his. Tabitha began speaking to William, saying, "It breaks my heart to have to tell you this."

However, Tabitha didn't get to finish her statement as a familiar voice spoke and asked, "It's going to break your heart to tell William what?"